THE TROUBLE WITH PARENTS

A Campus Life Book

THE TROUBLE WITH PARENTS

HOW TO MAKE PEACE WITH YOURS

Edited by
Tim Stafford

Designed by
Joan Nickerson

ZONDERVAN PUBLISHING HOUSE
OF THE ZONDERVAN CORPORATION
GRAND RAPIDS, MICHIGAN 49506

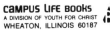
CAMPUS LIFE BOOKS
A DIVISION OF YOUTH FOR CHRIST
WHEATON, ILLINOIS 60187

We are grateful to the publishers of the following for permission to reprint material appearing in this book:

"Three-Way Love" is adapted from the book *People Lovers* by William S. Taegel, published by Word Books, © 1972.

"The Five Biggest Hassles" is from the book *Outside Disneyland* by Jay Kesler and Tim Stafford, published by Word Books, © 1977.

"Surviving a Divorce" by Larry Lewis is reprinted from *Insight*, a Christian youth magazine published by Seventh-day Adventists, © 1974, Review and Herald Publishing Association, Washington, D.C. 20012.

THE TROUBLE WITH PARENTS
Copyright © 1978 by Youth for Christ International

Library of Congress Cataloging in Publication Data

Main entry under title:

The Trouble with parents.

    "A Campus life book."
    1. Parent and child—Addresses, essays, lectures.
    2. Family—Addresses, essays, lectures.   I. Stafford, Tim.
HQ755.85.T76   301.42'7   78-13597
ISBN 0-310-32961-2

Printed in the United States of America

Contents

Foreword

You have probably never seen a book quite like this one. If you've thumbed through it, by now you know that there are photos and many short chapters written by different authors.

Many books on parents begin with a verbal blueprint of what a family should be like. Then they offer advice on how you can fit in. There is one author, one perspective, one blueprint for every family . . . and one sermon that applies to everyone.

We don't think that's quite fair. Families are different. The people who constitute them are very different, with diverse problems and needs. How can you lump them all together?

The Trouble With Parents is designed to reflect the varied realities that make up families. The book has a number of writers, and while their views don't conflict, each one offers a different flavor and perspective. They give advice, but they also offer thought-provoking viewpoints, personal stories, models of families they've seen working and failing.

This book contains a wealth of information. But it will not spell out for you exactly how you are to get along with your parents. Rather, you will have to think about how each chapter applies, or fails to apply, to your situation. You'll find yourself, we hope, going back to some of the articles to read them over. We hope you'll also frequently find yourself putting down the book just to look into space and think. And, of course, we hope the insights will prod you into action.

One statement does fairly apply to all families: they matter. Shrug your shoulders and try to divorce yourself completely from them, and you will fail. There is probably no factor more crucial to your success as a person—not your grades or popularity or success at sports. Your parents affect you more than anyone.

—Tim Stafford, for the editors
of *Campus Life*

Why Are These People Scared?

They are your parents.
They have been taught (as you have)
not to show fear. Instead, they nag you
or act tough. But at heart's center
they are afraid. You scare them. Why?

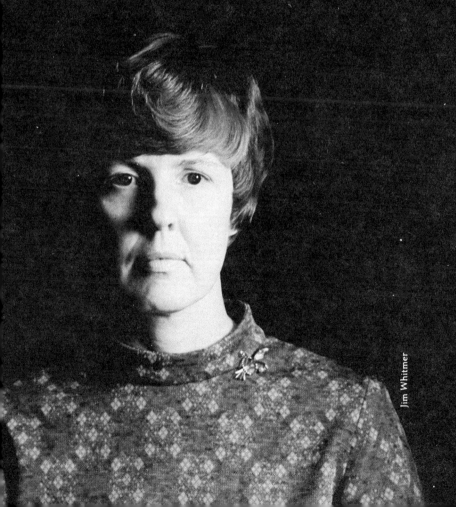

They are scared because you are getting away from them. They wanted you in the first place, and in their planning you would be their baby. You lived up to that at first. No matter how much you were a crying pain, you were theirs. You needed them, even to eat. They cuddled you, encircled you with their arms, and thought you were a little doll.

Now you're shattering their conception. You point out what they would rather forget: they chose you but you never chose them. You may love them (they hope you do) but you don't belong to them. You are getting away; and though they know better, they fear they soon will be rejected.

They are scared because you won't make up for their failures. By now they know that some of the things they wanted to do will never be done. They will never be famous. They will never be comfortably rich. They will never again be good-looking. They will die unmarked, part of a list in the newspaper, one of a few thousand who died that day.

And by now they have transferred their hopes to you. Why do you think they care how you look? Why do you think they care what grades you get? Why do you think they care about your friends?

They want you to do for yourself what they will never be able to do for themselves. And they're scared you won't.

Jim Whitmer

They are scared because they know how easy it is to waste your life.

They know, by experience, that there are three wrong directions for every one that's right.

Half their friends are unhappy. Are they, too? They don't want that for you.

But they know how easily it slips up; a casual decision to stick with the wrong friends, wrong habits, wrong thinking.

So they are scared, and they worry about you.

All right, you're stronger than they think. You're confident, but they're afraid. You know where you're going and they're not so sure. You don't have to absorb their fear, but can you respect it?

They are scared because they can't talk to you.

They love you, and that love forms words that stick to their tongues.

They want to share the stories of their life with you, but they are tales from another century about aunts and uncles you never knew. You don't laugh at their jokes.

They want to tell you what you mean to them, but they're embarrassed and you're busy doing homework.

They want to give you good advice, but the TV is on and who can talk?

They're afraid that you, the one they love, have left them behind and they won't be able to talk to you again. They want to talk, but how?

David S. Strickler

What's

It's mystifying. Having lived all your
to be much like them. You like the
most TV shows. If they're nervous,
has developed so as to be similar to
most of your life you probably got
☐Suddenly they are squelching the
want you to grow up. Can't they see
Why do they insist
☐And why do they have such an
you can't shrug off their opinions,
☐Where did all this trouble come
☐That's exactly the question your
something wrong? Or do they have a
☐The first step in understanding the
a big transition is going on—a
tension. When there is tension,
come out. So do many emotions. We
counsels dozens of shattered families

the Trouble?

life with these people, you've grown
same food. You probably agree on
you probably are too: your personality
theirs. You even look like them. For
along pretty well.
life out of you. It's like they never
you are able to take care of yourself?
on all those rules?
ability to drive you crazy? Why is it
their remarks?
from?
parents ask, too. Did they do
kid who's abnormal?
trouble with parents is to realize that
transition that normally creates
peoples' strengths and weaknesses
asked a practicing psychiatrist who
to trace that tense transition.

The Bloody War of Independence

by Penny Smith, M.D.

■We psychiatrists see an unusual side of life, and often the problems are exaggerated. Some kids who come to see me blurt out feelings which they have never told anyone else. Others are so scared and shy at first that I can't get them to say a complete sentence. It's pretty rare for a teenager to come to me on his own. Usually mom or dad has encouraged him, which automatically puts two strikes against me.

I see a variety of problems in teenagers, but almost all have one thing in common. They're all bloody, bandaged victims of the "War of Independence." That war is a conflict required of just about everyone who grows up, and usually it's waged against the parent.

You get hurt, not because you or your parents have severe problems, but because you're caught in a war

The battlefields change over the years. Now it's things like drugs and sexuality, whereas at another time hair length or skirt length set the grounds of conflict.

When I can bring a teenager to the place where he opens up, he usually says something like this: "Is there *any* way you can get my mom and dad to understand?" He's almost pleading. There's a brick wall ten feet thick between him and his parents.

Unfortunately, I usually must reply, "Probably not. I doubt they'll ever understand." Parents have simply forgotten what it was like when they went through the War of Independence.

It's too bad we have to use analogies like war to describe the process. It's really a natural growth process that we adults ought to learn to accept. Every person has to go through a stretching, expanding period when he finds his own identity, apart from his parents.

An infant's life is totally dependent on his parents. Even through grade school and junior high, most of a kid's life is determined for him by others: teachers, parents, youth directors. They set rules for him, tell him what he should learn and believe, what decisions he should make. But suddenly, in a brief period, the kid has to prepare himself to make all his own decisions and find out who he is and what he wants to be like. No wonder the battlefield gets a little smoky sometimes.

Can parents ever understand what kids are going through? Many are very wise and understanding and know how to handle signs of growth or independence. But the kids I counsel usually come from homes where the parents simply cannot cope with the situation, and the kid is totally trapped.

It's interesting that the Bible records only one event from Jesus' growing-up years. He was twelve years old and had gone to the temple with His parents. His mother and father took off on the journey home, assuming Jesus was with them, but suddenly they found that He was missing. Frightened, and probably angry, they rushed back to the temple and saw Jesus calmly holding court with the scholars. Can't you just imagine Mary's anxiety? "Son, do You realize what You put me through? I was worried sick!"

But Jesus understood the War of Independence. He knew His parents would have to adjust to a new scene as He grew up, and He could handle situations like that. Note Jesus' reaction. He didn't sulk or throw a tantrum. He obeyed His parents and went with them.

By the time you're a teenager, your parents have been looking after you for thirteen years. You can't expect them to let go of those strings overnight. It takes time and understanding, from both parties.

Psychologists who study teenagers are finding out there are vast differences between the ways teenagers and adults think and respond. The teenager's brain undergoes dramatic changes. He begins to use his brain for what scientists call "formal operations." For the first time he can logically manipulate thought and therefore, quite naturally, the teenager spends a lot of time inside his own head—thinking, figuring things out.

Parents, on the other hand, see their kid as being spacy and lazy. But you have to understand where the parents are coming from. They are concerned with survival. What's on your dad's mind on any given day? His job satisfaction, rising prices, insurance bills, planning for your college, tensions with your mother. Your mother is probably concerned with feeding you, raising your brothers and sisters, taking care of relatives. If she works, her task is doubly complex.

Moreover, most parents are plain scared. They've never dropped acid or smoked pot, but they read in *Time* magazine about the high percentages of kids who do. They read the statistics of kids who have sex and of the hundreds of thousands of unwed mothers, and they're scared to death about you.

These are some of the reasons I say, "No, I can't cross that communication barrier between you and your parents." I don't think there can be perfect, clear understanding between parents and teenagers. You're coming from two different sets of pressures and tensions.

So, if you feel your parents don't understand you—relax. Join the millions. You probably don't understand your parents either.

Is the situation hopeless? I've seen too many happy families to believe that. I think the biggest lesson a kid can learn is to accept and care for his parents even when there is no communication. Too often, when problems arise the teenager sulks or refuses to talk or won't cooperate around the house. Maybe he starts acting deliberately rebellious, antagonizing his parents. That's a dead end. My advice is to keep on trying to be understanding even when you're not getting through to your parents.

When is the last time you expressed interest in your dad's job or in your parents' friends? When is the last time you asked about their hobbies or the vacations they took before you came along? Kids can hold the key to their parents' sense of self-worth. Parents have invested an awful lot in you—are they seeing any return on their investment?

Your parents *will* fail you. That's a revolutionary thought to most kids. Often the most rebellious kids, who really hurt their parents, are plagued with tremendous guilt feelings. It's been hammered into them all their life that their parents are always right, and when differences erupt they feel it's their fault. It's more likely to be a mutual problem.

What kind of homes do work? The most important ingredient I've seen is unconditional love. A parent should communicate to his kids that he loves and accepts them *regardless.* Fill in anything you want— the kid can run away, sin grossly, reject everything the parent stands for—but the teenager has to believe his parents will love him no matter what. Jesus' parable of the prodigal son, as told in Luke 15, is the best example here.

Only in the family can you find that kind of love. James Dobson describes in his book *Hide or Seek* how you rate in our society. He says society gives a gold coin of self-respect if you're beautiful. You get a silver coin if you have a lot of brains. And you get a bronze coin of self-respect for having money. The family should be directly opposed to that sort of value rating. You are valuable because you were born. You belong to your family simply because you exist. And no matter how irritating you think your situation is, it's unlikely you'll find any other group in society that genuinely accepts you as freely as your family accepts you. If your parents are wise enough to love you in spite of anything and everything, you stand a chance of surviving the War of Independence without wounds.

You too have a responsibility. You must love and accept your parents no matter what. No matter how boorish or unjust or cruel they appear to you, if you respond with love and maturity, God has promised to honor that response. ■

THE TROUBLE WITH PARENTS

Feelings

You *know* how you feel. But your
People who knew everything and told
them getting their feelings hurt,
worrying what you think of them.
upset as you do about how hard it is
what this trouble feels like to them, it
☐ The next five chapters are designed
your parents. It is information adults
secret the fact that you sometimes
the cafeteria, looking for
☐ Once you begin to understand the
can imagine how life seems to them
intelligently for a way to work

parents have always been those Big
you what to do. It's hard to imagine
feeling shy trying to talk to you, or
They do. And they get at least as
to get along. Until you can imagine
is going to be hard to communicate.
to let you in on the inside feelings of
usually keep secret—just as you keep
feel lost and afraid going into
friends to eat lunch with.
secret fears of your parents, once you
right now, you can begin to look
together.

Treating a Friend Like a Father

by Tim Stafford

■*I read somewhere that you should treat your parents with all the respect, patience, and understanding you would have toward your best friend.*

"That is how I have always treated them," I said to myself. But when I thought about it, I wasn't so sure. I went on a little daydream excursion, wondering what it would be like if my best friend, Ernie Estabrook, came over, and . . .

"Hi," Ernie said. "Are you ready to go to the basketball game?"

"Would you get off my back?" I said in my most exasperated tone. "You're always rushing me. What difference does it make if we're a little late?"

Ernie shrugged. "None, I guess. What did you do this afternoon?"

"Nothing," I grunted.

"Did you have practice after school?"

"Nah."

"You came straight home?"

"Yeah."

"So what did you do?"

A brief daydream in which my friend Ernie turned into someone else

"Nothing!" I exploded. "Why do you always pry into my private life?"

"Sorry," Ernie said. He looked a little hurt and tried to change the

25

subject. "Hey, I saw you talking to Charlotte today. How do you rate? She's really something, isn't she?"

"Look, let's make an agreement," I said. "You let me make my own friendships. I'm mature enough to know who I want to be friends with and who I don't. I can't see that it's any of your business."

"Hey, I was just trying— Aw, forget it. Let's go to the game."

"I'll be ready in a minute," I said. "Can I have five bucks?"

"Well, I don't know," Ernie said doubtfully. "I don't have much money. Don't you have any money of your own?"

"Where would I get it?" I asked sarcastically. "I suppose you want me to get a job on top of a full day at school and playing in the band."

"Who said anything about a job?"

"Everyone always wants you to get terrific grades and practically be an Einstein, but they won't lend you the money to go to a basketball game and relax once in a while. I suppose you'd prefer I went out drinking. That's cheaper, you know. It wouldn't cost you a cent."

"Forget I said anything," Ernie said. "You can have the money. Let's just go to the game. We're late already."

"You're *always* pushing me," I grumbled on the way out the door. But I stopped. "Ernie, do we have to go in that crummy car? It looks so *old!* Everyone else drives a new car, and I have to go in that beat-up refugee from a junkyard. Can't you get something new?"

"I would if I had the money," Ernie mumbled.

"That's the trouble with you," I said. "All you think about is money. You're always so worried about spending a little bit extra. You're so tied up in cash, you don't take time to think about more meaningful things."

"I guess you're right," Ernie said, his head down.

"You bet I'm right," I said. "And if you think I'm going to sit with you at the game, you're crazy!"

At this point in my daydream my father walked into the room. I took my feet off the coffee table, sat up straight, and said, "Hi, dad. How did your day go?"

"Now what do you want?" he sighed. ∎

THE TROUBLE WITH PARENTS

Memoirs of an Adult

as told to Steve Lawhead

■An adult is something you've wanted to be ever since you found out there was such a thing. But how much do you really know about adults? Not much, I'll bet. The reason is, most adults are afraid to spill their guts. They don't want to look weak or silly—especially in front of kids. Therefore you get a false picture of what being an adult is like.

I'm going to try to give you the inside story, because I think you ought to know. This isn't pleasant stuff, but it's the true story of my life as an adult. I'll show you where I live, my family, and my friends. I'll start with my neighborhood—typically suburban, clean, orderly, ordinary people.

How much do you really know about being an adult?

In the house to the left of me is a family in which the husband travels about five nights a week. Until recently, the wife had to work to help pay the mortgage. Then she found out she had cancer

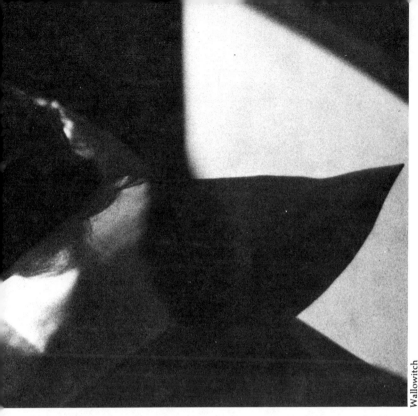

Wallowitch

and went in for an operation that at first seemed successful. Two or three months later she went back for an examination only to find cancer in a completely different part of her body. The doctors concluded that her body has somehow gained the ability to produce cancer and, needless to say, there are some tensions in the home.

In the house across the street a thirty-five-year-old married woman is living with a twenty-two-year-old single guy. She has kids in junior high school and they don't get to see their real father much—he comes around only every two or three weeks and then goes off again. He doesn't complain about his wife's arrangement, because he is living with his twenty-two-year-old friend.

Next to them is a house that was ordinarily very peaceful and quiet. The family kept pretty much to themselves until a few weeks ago. We were awakened in the middle of the night by a noise like a screen door slamming loudly and a little later the sounds of angry voices outside. I looked out the bedroom window to discover the strobing light of four police cars lined up on the lawn across the street. Being a nosy neighbor, I donned my bathrobe and went out to see what was happening. The father was being taken out in handcuffs, and the police threw him in the backseat of one of their cars. The kids stood by the car beating on the glass with their fists and cursing him. Seconds later, their mother was carried out on a stretcher and hurried to an ambulance. She had been shot by her husband in an argument over who got the house in their divorce.

Next door to them is a family whose son is in college. When he brings his pals home to visit, he tells his folks to put a couple of extra beds in the basement because they pick up girls to spend the night with. The parents say, "Well, that's the way kids are today."

Down the block, another neighbor—Charlie—is happy he can walk. His left leg is almost totally paralyzed, a reminder that a few years ago he barely escaped a very slow, agonizing death. Doctors stood by helplessly as a paralysis started in his legs and slowly worked its way up his body to his neck. It stopped at his chin. Then, just as mysteriously, recovery slowly worked its way down until the paralysis remained only in his left leg. Being an old race driver, Charlie likes to work on his car. It sometimes takes him an hour just to hoist himself under the car, but he's happy even to be able to move.

Another neighbor is a golf pro. He gets drunk now and then and stays at the club, often not coming home for three or four nights in a row.

A few doors down on the other side of the street lives a surgeon who hasn't been out of his bedroom for two years. He has a disease that resembles multiple sclerosis and refuses treatment because he thinks it's incurable. His nine-year-old daughter brings him food to keep him alive. This little girl writes pathetic little notes to my own daughter saying: "Do you love me? (A) More than Joanie? (B) Just a little bit? (C) Less than Sally? or, (D) Not as much as anyone?"

In the house behind us lives a couple who are both doctors. They work all the time, so when their junior-high daughters come home alone they bring the boys and take them up to their bedrooms to play "Check out the bod." So far they have been able to get away with it, or else the parents don't mind.

That's my neighborhood. I don't think it is untypical—it's just that the average person doesn't always know what's going on.

THE TROUBLE WITH PARENTS

Now then, here's my family:

My dad has had two severe heart attacks. After open-heart surgery, he recovered only to struggle with Parkinson's disease. My mother is not much better off: she also has heart problems.

My brother was okay until he got into college. At football practice one day, while running a simple pass pattern, he accidentally collided head-on with another player. The other guy was shorter than he, so his helmet smashed full in my brother's face. Ken received a severe concussion and a fractured jaw. When my mother saw him, she didn't even recognize him. He lay helpless in the college infirmary for some time: the doctors were unable to move him to adequate facilities because a dislodged blood clot would have killed him.

I had a cousin who was a highly successful state senator down south. Eventually the pressure of home and office got to him, and he drove his Cadillac into a cement abutment at seventy-five miles per hour, committing suicide.

There are many more examples, of course, but this is a small sample of the world adults live in. It's different from a young person's ideas about it, I know. My life once centered around homework, rock 'n' roll, and a Friday night game with a date. But that changes eventually—it has to —and you wouldn't want it any other way. Can you imagine having the same interests and ambitions at forty that you did at fourteen? Yet, even though becoming an adult is a desirable thing, I feel the weight of my age. As I get older, I think about the people around me and their problems and I think that maybe I am a candidate for all these things. They all contribute to my fear of the world.

There's the fear of failure. Vocational success is considered very important in America. I find I must continually work to secure myself in my job because being a success is expected of me. And as the economy goes from bad to worse, my security gets shakier and shakier. My family's needs weigh heavier on me. If I lose my job, that means I've failed myself and my family and I can't provide for them—there goes my security right out the window. I must not fail.

Then there is the fear of old age. The commercial says, "When you've got your health—you've got just about everything." Well, I know that as I grow older, my health is going to weaken. I don't always recover as quickly from the aches and pains of life as I used to. The little touch-football game with the kids last Saturday left me stiff and sore for a week. One day I must look in the mirror and realize the body that has been carrying me around all these years is disintegrating. Every day when I wake up, I know that I am less than the person I was yesterday. This produces severe mental tension.

Next, I look around and see there are things I'm never going to get a chance to do. When I was a kid, I wanted to be a pro baseball player; I realize now I can never play for the Dodgers. I once wanted to travel the world and see foreign places; now, with my family growing up, I know I will never have enough money to make that dream come true.

The opportunities I have are diminishing. Every day something passes that I can never return to. I feel stuck in my position at work, but I know that if I quit and look for something better, I might never get another job. I'm getting too old for someone to hire—and I'm only thirty-five!

My children, though I love them dearly, cause me fear. I watch them growing further and further away from me. I wonder what will become of them. Will they remain true to the things I've tried to teach them, or drift away, embarrassing me?

I'm afraid for my self-worth. Society doesn't need me to get along. I'm worth something only as long as what I *do* is worth something to society. Slowly I am working myself out of a place in society just by getting older.

And finally, there's the fear of death. As I get older, I begin outliving certain others of my family and friends. Every year a few more die, either from health reasons or from accidents or injury. My grandparents die off, and then my own parents. Finally, I'm the last link on the family chain—and then I'll drop off.

If, as an adult, I am difficult to understand, it is probably because I am just trying to survive as a person. It takes all the energy I have just to keep going. In *Through the Looking Glass,* Alice came to a place in Wonderland where she had to run as fast as she could just to stay in the same place, and twice as fast if she wanted to get anywhere—I feel like that sometimes. Sometimes I don't have enough emotional energy left to help myself, let alone my wife or kids—or my neighborhood.

I do not think that the pressures an adult faces are any greater than the kinds of pressures a high-schooler faces. I'm not saying that

THE TROUBLE WITH PARENTS

adults are in a pressure cooker and the kids have it easy. I'm saying that there is a different kind of pressure, and the difference is this: for a high-school kid there is always hope. If he's not popular he can play the game and next month he can have longer hair, new clothes, a bigger this or lesser that—then he'll be popular. The future is always bright. There are better things to look forward to.

The possibility of good things happening in the future makes it easier for a high-school kid to cope. Being jilted by her boy friend may be just as heavy for a kid as all the pressures on an adult, but one short month later that same girl will feel terrific because there's a new guy. Yet, for an adult, the tensions of permanent illness, death, a broken marriage—none of these things leave. And the older he gets, the more of them there are.

I am not trying to scare you to make you say, "I don't want to get any older—it's depressing." I am trying to show you that adults are human beings too. They need understanding like everyone else. We are more like you than we are different, and our fears and tensions get to us just as yours do. I think if all of us—adults and kids together—understand this, we can help each other.

And although I have painted a gloomy picture of adult life, I think it's safe to say that for every adult who has failed, many more have found the way to handle their adulthood. I could write an article three times as long as this one about the joys of being an adult. Instead, I've given you this one-sided treatment which should help you realize adults are vulnerable; we hurt sometimes and, like you, we need others to help us with our problems. Understanding an adult's problems is where a kid can really help out—using kind understanding will help release some of the tension on the adults around you.

Much depends on *your* attitude. If you expect your parents, teachers, or other adults to be invincible supermen, you will always be negative toward them, because they won't measure up. But if you consider the fact that they might be lonely, frightened individuals, then your response to them may be just what they need. And what is more, when you become an adult you will understand yourself a little better. ■

Those Annoying, Smothering, Uptight Parents

by Philip Yancey

■ Both the students and parents were nervous. A church in Napa, Idaho, had thrown them together for a weekend retreat. The kids banded together, defensive. So did the parents.

The first evening, the two groups were separated. Parents went off to watch a film, while Campus Life Director Don Mardock stayed with the crowd of teenagers in a bare room with two oversized blackboards. "We're going to do something you may have wanted to do for a long time," he began. "For the next thirty minutes, I want you to come up with every gripe you can think of against your parents."

What exactly bugs parents? It's not what you think

Kids once quiet and bored snapped to attention. A few smart alecks tried to be clever: "My mother wants my room to look like a suite in the Waldorf Hotel" or "My dad hasn't been wrong about anything since second grade." But before long, the emotional tone had changed. Serious, pent-up tensions came out, and Don patiently wrote each one on the blackboard:

"My parents don't trust me."

"They never admit they're wrong."

"They don't listen."

"They want to live their lives through me."

When the half-hour ended, Don had completely filled the huge blackboard with more than forty major gripes.

Then Don rolled the covered blackboard against the wall, and the kids switched places with their parents upstairs. After explaining the procedure, Don was immediately deluged with parents' gripes about kids:

"Kids have no understanding of the pressures I go through."

"I live in the suburbs for *their* safety and they blame me for being racially prejudiced!"

"How can I trust my kids when they've done nothing to earn trust?"

"My son's had three traffic tickets and two accidents, and he sulks when I don't give him the car."

"Mine are moody."

In a few minutes, Don had filled half of the second board, and hands were still popping up. He spotted one distraught-looking lady with her hand propped up and pointed to her. "Don," she began in an unsteady voice, "why are we enjoying this so much? Look at the things up there—pressure, irresponsibility, lack of trust, no communication. Who are we trying to fool? Those things are just as true of us as they are of our kids."

Silence. A few parents nodded agreement; others spoke out. "She's right, Don. Our kids have problems, but they're not that different from ours. We're not perfect." After a lot of dicussion, the parents asked Don to erase all twenty of the gripes they had so eagerly contributed. Instead, they wrote on the board a single sentence that summarized their one most important gripe.

After Don had wheeled that blackboard against the wall, the teenagers piled back into the same room, sitting across from their parents. They were chattering, enthusiastic about the chance to charge their parents with whatever bugged them, no holds barred.

Don rolled out the blackboard full of gripes against parents. He randomly asked kids in the group to explain. One by one, kids stood up and gave examples of how cold, unresponsive, and unreasonable their parents were. The parents sat in silence, listening to eloquent explanations of all forty gripes. Some kids were funny, some

THE TROUBLE WITH PARENTS

emotional, but everyone got across a pointed criticism.

Now for the parents. The kids were excited, spoiling for a fight, ready to blast whatever the parents had written. Don wheeled the board around. In large letters was written this one sentence: "The one thing we don't like about our kids is that they're too much like we are."

Total silence. A lot of thinking, some tears, and one-on-one communication followed. It lasted far into the night. ■

Image/Michael Hayman

A Ripping of Fabric

by Harold Myra

■ I was full of excitement as I stuffed my Datsun with suitcases, a typewriter, and books. From a small town in the Pennsylvania mountains I was traveling to Chicago. New challenges. New friends.

My parents shared my enthusiasm. Together we had a commitment to Christ. We respected and loved each other. I would miss them.

But my brain was on Chicago, and my emotions flowed toward the future. I was intent on new worlds.

They sent letters several times a week. At Christmas and Easter they welcomed me as if I had come home from East Asia. And I liked that.

But what did they really feel?

You're leaving home— why do your parents look pained?

I got a hint not long after I left home. I met Jeanette in Wisconsin and took her to Pennsylvania at Christmastime. I put the ring on her finger and we walked into the kitchen and made our announcement.

Amid all the congratulations and smiles and joy sneaked in the words, "Well, Harold, you didn't get your girl from Pennsylvania, did you?" It was meant to be humorous, a side remark, filler. But it came up out of a deep yearning. A Wisconsin girl meant less chance I'd live nearby. Why did they have to think about that?

Only one way would I understand: later, Jeanette and I had a baby girl, Michelle. And then a little boy, Todd.

How can I describe my emotions toward them? Holding them. Talking to them. Throwing them into the air. If anything happened to them, it would slice deep. I love them like . . . like I love Jeanette.

And I guess that's the parallel.

I used to dream of finding *the* girl. Building a life together. Enjoying each other. Planning together for a lifetime. I always knew that, once in love, breaking apart would be like sawing me in half.

And now, it's the same with Michelle and Todd. Until I was a dad myself, I never dreamed my love for them would be as strong as my love for Jeanette. Or that breaking from them would be as tough in some ways as seeing Jeanette walk away from me.

Oh, I don't intend to become a clinging parent. Mine weren't. But as Todd and Michelle grow toward all the excitement of their futures, they won't feel what I will: this oneness with them. They will be all wrapped up in college or engagements or career.

So I'm psyching myself to enjoy freeing them a little at a time, then to enjoy watching them fly from the nest with strong wings. Sure, I'll smile and laugh and share their enthusiasm as they leave. But I don't expect them to look back and understand my feelings. I didn't a few years ago. I had to get this bond with Michelle and Todd to understand what my parents felt the day I packed that Datsun. Their tears mixed with their hugs and handshakes meant more than a warm ritual—it was a ripping of fabric, like birth ripping through the living tissue of the mother.

It's natural—the mixture of pain and joy. But somehow I wish I had understood all that the day I hugged mom and dad good-by.■

Do They

"They love me? Well, they sure
□Yes, they do have a funny way of
to show love. But most parents do love
them so. They have a unique language
□No doubt your parents could find
care about you. (Maybe you could find
love for *them*, too.) But in the
least *some* comfort to realize that beneath
commentary on what's wrong with the
□The next four chapters decipher
to read their everyday actions, the

Love You?

have a funny way of showing it. . . ."
showing it. It is hard for some people
their kids and are constantly telling
you need to learn to understand.
better language to let you know they
better ways of communicating your
meantime, it will have to do. It is at
their nagging, their rules, and their
world today is a genuine love for you.
part of the language. If you can learn
message is quite clear.

The
Money Talks

■Ever feel cheap? You're actually an expensive investment. Time, love, energy, worry—those things are too hard to calculate. Think just of the stacks of crinkled green bills your parents have dished out on account of you.

At least they paid $54,938 for you

Obviously, family budgets differ, and this list may not apply to you. If so, figure up your own list. We're figuring for a senior in high

43

school. After that it gets worse—$21,000 for college, $2,000 for a wedding . . .

The First Year

Getting born (hospital, doctor, etc.)	$1,200	Medical care	400
Baby wardrobe	100	Tonsillectomy	400
Nursery furnishing	100	Dentist (twice a year, $20 each trip)	240
Feeding equipment	40	Toys, games and extra goodies	600
Miscellaneous (vitamins, diaper service)	100	Special extra-lavish toy	100
Medical care after birth	200	Piano lessons (once a week starting at age 8)	1,200
Food	250	Piano for above	1,000
Housing	720	Figure skating	600
Clothing	94	Summer camp (ages 8 to 11 three weeks)	700
Toys	150	Baby-sitting	2,500
Silver spoon	13	Family dog (purchase price)	100
Baby's nest egg (beginning savings account)	100	Shots and yearly vet fees ($50 a year)	300
Photographing baby professionally	100	Dog food ($80 a year)	480

Babyhood (1-5: five years)

Food (U.S.D.A. figures)	2,000
Housing ($720 x 5)	3,600
Furnishing kid's room	100
Clothing	900
Medical care	350
Dentist (once a year, $20 each trip)	100
Nursery school or kindergarten	2,000
Toys	600
Baby-sitting	2,000
Two special birthday parties	50
Vacations	250

Adolescence (12-17: six years)

Food	4,000
Housing	4,320
Clothing	2,000
School supplies and extra fees	600
Medical expenses	375
One major injury (broken leg or equivalent)	300
Dentist	350
Orthodontia	2,000
Summer camp through age 15	800
One special trip each year (bike hike, etc.)	300
Toys, games, sports and goodies	920
10-speed bike	100
Electric guitar and piano lessons	400

Childhood (6-11: six years)

Food	3,000
Housing	4,320
Re-do child's room at age 9	300
Clothing ($215 a year)	1,290

Kid takes up skiing	225	Camera (serviceable 35mm.)	100
School projects	200	Film and developing (one roll a month at $4)	288
Teenage ski vacation every other year	600	Dog (continued). Shots and vet $50 a year	300
Spectator sports	100	Dog food	480
Special events (rock concerts, etc.)	160	Use of TV	120
Use of telephone	150	Haircuts	126
Room refurnished and decorated	400	Watch (cheap)	25
		Cosmetics, starting at 13	200
Allowance, $2 a week	672	Gas in family car	150
Stereo phonograph	250	Insurance (16 and 17)	400
Records (one a month for six years at $3.89)	280	Vacations	600
			$54,938

You Think We're Crazy?

Well, consider this. Your mother has probably lost fifteen years of possible employment taking care of you. The 1969 Commission on Population Growth and the American Future figured the lost "opportunity costs" of a non-working mother at $6,762 a year. If that's what your mother's worth, in fifteen years it adds up to $101,430! So you actually cost closer to $200,000. ■

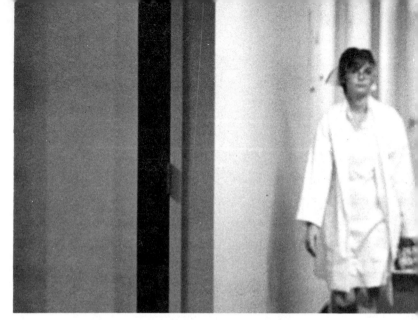

Visit a Hospital

■ Start at the maternity ward. Behind a glass case you will see row after row of shriveled, red babies, squirming feebly and crying in unison. Look closely. Their eyes are swollen shut, their foreheads are dented from forceps, their hair is thin and scattered. Not very appealing. If you saw such a product in a Sears catalog, you'd quickly flip the page.

Now go to a room where new parents are holding that wrinkled red baby. Surprise! They are gurgling and laughing and poking it and ex-

The truth comes out in a crisis

claiming about how beautiful—yes, *beautiful!*—it is. And they're serious! The woman you see has just spent the most agonizing day of her life, tearing flesh and muscle to push that baby out, and she's absolutely convinced that every thrust of pain was worth it.

But don't stop with the maternity ward. Go on to intensive care and ask to see the rooms where teenagers stay. One or two will be suffering from car accidents. Puffy scars crisscross their faces, and plastic tubes spill from their noses, throats, and abdomens. Perhaps a girl is there due to a fall from a horse. One is dying of cancer.

Jim Whitmer

by Philip Yancey

You may not be able to see the kids, but in the waiting room you will see the parents. They're always there. Come back in five, ten, or twenty hours: they will be waiting. Nothing else in the world matters to them but that bruised hunk of tissue kept alive by plastic tubes. The father may be working two jobs, paying out $150 per day to keep his daughter alive. The mother has dropped out of everything: she goes to no meetings, she sees no friends. Her life is the hospital. Maybe she and her kid fought often—that doesn't matter now. She will be there, waiting. She will be the first face her daughter sees if she finally regains consciousness. She will devote months to her recovery. She will clean the bed, bathe her, cheer her up, buy her presents—anything. Nothing else matters.

Hospitals show parents at their best.

But perhaps the nitty-gritty of living with teenagers shows them at their worst.

Your parents may seem unwise, confused, out-of-date (just as you will seem to your kids some day). At those times, what helps most is to believe—*really believe*—that they love you. If you ever doubt that, there is one easy cure—visit a hospital. ∎

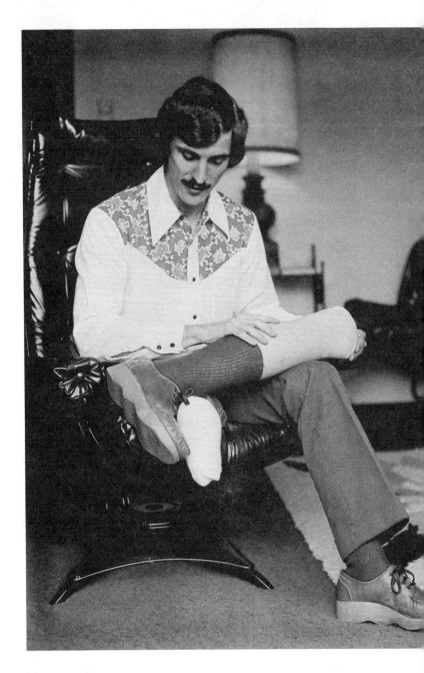

Every Year a New Leg

by Pat Vance

■ I was about five years old when I first realized that not everyone took off his right leg before getting into the bathtub. Because of a birth defect, my leg had been amputated when I was seven months old. There was no bone below the knee, so the foot and ankle were useless. Doctors recommended early amputation, since the leg would never develop properly.

There were times of self-pity, but I can't really say I had an abnormal childhood. My artificial leg caused some strange, even humorous events. During a kickball game in elementary school, my leg came unattached at the very moment I kicked the ball. It flew

Some prefer silent ways of saying 'I love you'

all the way to the pitcher's mound. Another time I took a step and my leg came off and clattered to the floor in the school hallway. When school began each fall, I would freak out the new kids by reaching down to adjust my socks and suddenly twisting my leg around backward.

Generally, people were kind and accepting about my condition. I could run and play sports, and as long as I wore long pants, it was difficult to tell I was an amputee. The roughest part was probably in Phys Ed. I was stuck in a class with kids with heart murmurs, asthma, and hernias. I couldn't wear shorts, because that made my leg obvious. And there were embarrassing moments in the locker room when someone new would find my leg in the locker while I was taking a shower.

Only one thing about my leg caused great pain: the operations. Bone kept growing and pushing against the flap of skin where my stump ended, causing inflammation. Then I could hardly walk, so fifteen separate times I went into the hospital and had the bone scraped back. It put me out of commission three months each time, and I would try to keep up with schoolwork by using private tutors.

My childhood might have been absolutely miserable, however, except for one person—my father. I was never that close to dad. He was an engineer, not a very vocal person, and he didn't express his emotions easily. He was fifty-two when I was born, and I can imagine the grief it caused him to have a deformed son after so many childless years of marriage.

When I came home from the hospital, dad examined the artificial limb they had fitted me with. It was a tiny wooden leg with a lacer around the thigh, and with shoulder and waist straps. Despite the harness, the leg would keep detaching. My mother says she cried when she saw the contraption, all rawhide and wood and steel wrapped around a tiny baby. I would have to be fully undressed just for a diaper change. Dad was sure I would never learn to walk with a device like that.

So my dad did an amazing thing. He quit his job as a space engineer and signed up for a one-year apprenticeship with a limb maker. He drew no salary that year. At that time, the artificial-limb business was using crude designs and materials. Limb makers worked with drawings, rather than plaster casts which would have shown the stress points better.

Dad made a plastic duplicate of my stump and experimented with Fiberglas and resin materials. He baked the socket for my stump in the kitchen oven, filling the house with a terrible odor.

But it worked! I was walking on dad's new leg design before I was ten months old. And dad never stopped tinkering. Each year he came out with an even more improved model. I needed a new leg often anyway, because my left leg was growing normally. His custom limbs required no straps and buckles to hold them on; they fit over my stump as easily as an old shoe fits over a foot.

Each year as I went through the physical and psychological strain of an operation, dad absorbed the financial strain. The operations cost $2,000 to $3,000 apiece. He never complained or tried to make me feel bad for causing so much work. If I ever had a problem, he would stay up all night in his shop, repairing my leg so I could wear it to school the next day.

As I said, dad and I were never especially close. Especially in my

THE TROUBLE WITH PARENTS

teenage years, we went through the typical hassles. I'm sure I didn't express love for him as I should have, and I'm sure I will never fully appreciate all he has sacrificed for me. Really, isn't that true of all kids and their parents?

I think that sometimes we overemphasize the "warm, furry feelings" side of love. We think there can't be love without an obvious emotional display. Many of my friends get hung up on that. Their parents don't really know how to relate to them; they seem distant and aloof, and my friends just assume their parents don't love them.

Well, I've concluded that parents show their love in many different ways. Sometimes it's through cleaning up after their kids have vomited all over the shag carpet. Sometimes it's through letting kids go out with people they really don't approve of, or through paying for a college education when they really want you to go to another school. And in my case, it's pretty obvious how dad showed his love to me. You can see the proof in file drawers full of designs and blueprints of my legs, and a whole workshop built to manufacture them. He's in his seventies now, still working, hoping to come up with an improved version next year. ∎

Never Letting Go

by George Lanning

■ I got my first "real" set of parents when I was fifteen. Before that I lived on the street, sleeping in parked cars, all-night laundromats, city parks, or at friends' homes. Once I lived with my baseball team's manager for three months, and another time I holed up in an empty football stadium.

I lived that way because my step-father beat me. Not for any reason I could determine. Often, after a beating, he would tell me, "Now that's for what you're *going* to do!" Meaning, I guess, that discipline was a kind of

Was there a reason behind the list of rules?

bank account in which he had to make deposits to cover my future withdrawals. I never understood what made him tick.

When I was twelve years old he told me to get out or he'd kill me. I didn't know if he was serious or not, and since my mother didn't offer to intervene (she was too afraid to stand up against him) I thought I would take the hint and get out.

So by the time I was fifteen I had seen much of the dirty undersides of life. And I had participated in some smear campaigns of my own—the dirt kind of rubs off on you.

I thought everyone lived like I did, in his own way. I thought that's what life was like. Until I met Kathy.

Kathy was the finest thing I had ever seen. She was smart and popular, with the kind of smile that would make you give up whatever might keep you from being with her. Most importantly, she liked me as much as I liked her.

She was "the girl" for me, forever. She was the first person I had ever known who cared about me; she put up with me in all my foul

53

Tim Stafford

moods and gross behavior. And I idolized her for it. Kathy was my best friend.

Kathy was a Christian and I hadn't known her very long before I found out what the inside of a church looked like. Her family went to church every Sunday. Seeing it as an opportunity to be near her, I went too. At the youth meetings on Sunday nights, I would be the first one there in the evening and the last to go home at night (usually because I didn't have any place to go at night anyway).

One Sunday the minister spoke on John 3:16. He asked us all to put our name in the verse, and I went along with it. I ran it through my mind: "For God so loved George Lanning that he gave his only Son, that if George Lanning believed in Him, he wouldn't die, but have eternal life." Something clicked in my mind and I knew God was calling me. I answered.

Kathy thought it was wonderful. She worked to keep me on the upward climb. Whenever my feet wandered from the "true path" (they wandered down every bend in the road), she brought me back. She kept me involved with school, church, and other people. She lavished more time and love on me than a dozen social workers could have.

Our church soon acquired a new music director who took over our evening youth meetings. One night after everyone else had gone home, he and I were locking up the place. "Where are you going to sleep tonight, George?" he asked matter-of-factly. He knew my situation since it was no big secret.

"The park, I guess," I told him. I hadn't given it much thought.

"No," he said, "you can stay with my wife and me tonight."

I stayed with them that night, and the next . . . and the next two months of nights. Clean sheets, my own bathroom, a kitchen with a refrigerator—I had it made. I was beginning to wonder how long a good thing could last when they decided to make it permanent. Legally it was no hassle; I had been deserted by my real family. So I was adopted, and my family was expanded by two. I was on top of the world, for a while at least.

You might say I had character flaws, rough edges I had picked up in the streets. What I had thought was normal, acceptable behavior, I began to see was not normal or acceptable in a family relationship.

My new parents began a full-time remaking process on me; I had to be cleaned and polished for society. One by one my quirks were

THE TROUBLE WITH PARENTS

ironed out—but not without a lot of pain.

Lying was one of the first flaws they tackled. Somehow I had gotten the idea that it didn't matter what you said when you talked to someone. When my parents asked me a question, I would tell them anything that came to mind—sometimes to cover up something I had done, but most often just to make conversation. Lies were all I knew. They got me in constant trouble; but too dumb to know any better, I stuck by them. I would lie even when there was no point in lying. When someone asked me what time it was I would look at my watch and tell them 5:00 when it was actually only 3:30. It was all the same to me.

But my new parents took a hard line on the matter. And it was strange to see how I reacted to it. In the past, if I had been caught lying, my stepfather would take his shoe and beat me around the room. I would cry, but inwardly I would spit in his eye and go right on lying.

It wasn't like that with my new father and mother. When they would look at me with that expression of hurt and disappointment —as if I had just muddied a sacred trust, or wasted the family income—I would melt. I couldn't stand up to that kind of concern. They loved me more than I could know, and *why* they did I never could guess.

Sometimes that love hurt.

I had been in and out of school, luckily more in than out, since the sixth grade. Education never had been one of my passions, and grades were merely something to keep teachers happy. They had nothing to do with me. My parents took another view.

When I was a junior in high school I learned I was failing algebra. I was going right down the tubes and couldn't have cared less. But my father had enough concern for both of us. He insisted I apply myself, insisted I could learn it, insisted I study—when that didn't work he called my algebra teacher and both of them ganged up on me. My teacher came by the house every morning before school and picked me up. I arrived a half-hour early and spent that time in his class, working with him on algebra. When the next round of grades came, I passed. No one was more amazed or pleased than I was.

I had to be helped in other areas, too. I was barely scraping by in many other subjects, and the reason was TV. It didn't matter what was on, if the TV was operable, I would watch it. I gave it my all.

Every spare minute went into TV watching.

But to show me that there was more to life than reruns, my folks severely restricted my viewing time. Often they had to be downright sneaky. They took to swiping the cord to the set whenever they left the house. I would howl, but there was nothing I could do about it. After a while I would settle down and hit the books.

Slowly I was learning the right way to live. Once in a while I would have a relapse, however. Every time I did something wrong my parents found out. It was uncanny. It wasn't as if they went around all the time checking up on me. They just had this unfailing sense, an antenna that picked up trouble. (They also knew most of the people in town—that helped.)

One time my parents had gone out for the evening. I had the place to myself, and to demonstrate that fact I decided to light up a cigarette, something I knew they disapproved of. I went to the bathroom and smoked my cigarette and didn't think anything more about it until my parents came home.

"What's burning?" my mother asked, sniffing around.

"It seems to be coming from the bathroom," said my father.

"Uh—I know, let's check it out," I volunteered. And we all three trooped into the bathroom and looked at the light fixtures and the ventilation system. Of course there was nothing there. "Oh, my friend Joey was over." I started making up a story to cover my embarrassment. "He started smoking and I told him to put it out, but he wouldn't. He must have come in here to finish it."

Nothing more was said about the matter. I thought I had handled the scene rather smoothly. I went on with my life like nothing had happened.

Later that week the church sponsored a banquet for all the high-school kids, a very big deal. We were all going to be dressed up, flowers for our dates, and all that. I had bought a new sports jacket and new slacks to match. Kathy had bought a dress and shoes, and was looking forward to the big event with great anticipation.

The whole thing fell apart when my parents announced I couldn't go. My life passed before my eyes. What had I done to deserve such heartache and sorrow? Then it hit me: the cigarette story. I had *lied* to them about the cigarette and they had found out. Lying had done me in again. Kathy cried when I told her.

Her parents were upset with me. My parents were upset with me.

The only person who wasn't upset with me was the banquet speaker who was staying at our house. Time was running out, but he convinced my parents to let me go to the banquet after all. I was elated—but then came the crusher. I could go to the banquet, but *without* Kathy. I was sick.

I called Kathy with the bad news and she took it hard, but agreed to make the best of it. She had an ace up her sleeve—another guy, whom she didn't particularly care for, had asked her at the last minute. She could accept a date with him and still go to the banquet. I would go alone and at least we'd be able to see each other.

I watched her across the room and all night long the only thing I could think of was, "Why did I have to lie to my parents?" The thought nagged me, haunting the banquet. I was miserable over my stupidity, and vowed never to lie to them again. The cost was too great.

I guess that was one incident where I learned another side to love. Love isn't merely saying nice things to someone, giving that person a warm, fuzzy feeling. Love can be tough. My parents loved me enough to do what they thought was best for me. I needed a lesson in love, and I got it.

My parents' concern was far-reaching. As important as that banquet was at that moment, my future was even more important. And they cared enough to keep the lines of communication open. Often my father would come to my room to just sit and talk things over with me. He'd put his arms around me and we'd cry if that was necessary, but we'd talk. Discipline to them was not a checking account, but a long-term investment: an investment in me. ■

It Can Get

You're not the only one who has
common than colds in January. But in
At least some people claim they've
let you experience families
Gut-level feelings come out, from
☐In small, subtle ways— and
—it's getting better for these people.
And it can reassure you you're not the

Better

trouble with parents. It's more
this disease, there is a possible cure.
found one. ☐ The next five chapters
working on living together.
deepest despair to high-flying elation.
sometimes in grand, booming ways
It can give you hope just to read.
only one with troubles.

My Shattered American Family

by Jake Currant

■ The arguments escalated during Christmas vacation. At first we could hardly detect what was wrong. Mom and dad would stare at each other over a meal, and not say much. Mom's eyes looked hurt and cloudy, and she avoided being in the same room with one of us kids alone, as if she were afraid we'd ask about something.

But by Christmas, no one was keeping any secrets. They stood in our living room, yelling at each other and arguing. Dad would wave his huge arms and shout; mom would say things like "How can you do this to me?" and sob. If one of us kids tried to butt in, dad would bark "Shut up and keep out of this."

You never know how much it means until you lose it

Three days after Christmas, mom left to stay with a friend. She came back in a couple of days, but it was too late. While she was gone, dad had decided to leave us for good. We found out there was another woman involved, and dad made it clear to us he preferred moving out to start a new life with a new family.

It was New Year's Day when he finally left. Snow was falling outside, and every family on the block was watching bowl games on TV. Sensing something big was about to happen, I stayed up in my room. Dad came in, laughed nervously and said, "Well, Jake old buddy, I'm leaving. This will make you grow—it'll be good for you." I didn't respond or follow him to the door, but a few seconds later the front door slammed shut and dad was gone.

Soon I could hear my younger brother, my older sister, and my mom in their rooms, all crying uncontrollably. I wanted to go to them, but I was too hurt myself. I just slumped on the bed and stared at the wall.

I can't express now—I can barely remember—the devastating

Image/Jack Corn

impact of the seven months following dad's leaving. My sister would be sitting in algebra, taking a pop quiz, and it would hit. She would start crying and have to leave the room. My mom was even weaker. I'm sure that if I had freaked out during those first months, mom would have had a nervous breakdown. She cried every day, for hours. I found myself in the weird position of having to help my mom emotionally by giving her strength. Suddenly there were no parents telling me what to do. I had to figure things out for myself, just to help our family survive. It was like being put in the driver's seat of a car, with no instructions or training, with people expecting me to start driving.

Some of my friends would say, "Yeah, Jake, I know how it is." They didn't. No one knows, unless he's been through it himself. I tried my best to act strong in front of mom. My only escape was to take long bike rides—sometimes fifty miles—and cry as I rode down the highway, tears blurring my vision. When I was finished crying I would stop at a gas station to wash my face, then head home.

I went through many stages. For a long time I kept hoping my father would come back, so we could all live together happily again. Slowly, I began to see how far-fetched that was. *Dad didn't want us—* that was the hardest part to accept.

In the middle of this period (I now call it the "seven months of hell") I found God. I gave my life to follow Jesus Christ after a Presbyterian youth group meeting. I started going to Campus Life club meetings in my high school in Cedar Rapids, Iowa, and counseled with Bob Shaffer, the director.

I can't say that God replaced what had been torn out of our family. That will never be replaced. But He did ease my loneliness. Mom became a Christian too. Sometimes, when we had nothing to say to each other which could possibly cheer us up, we would just read the Bible. I would turn to verses like Isaiah 41:10, "Fear not, for I am with you, be not dismayed, for I am your God; I will strengthen you, I will help you, I will uphold you with my victorious right hand" (RSV). Or we'd turn to a favorite chapter in the Book of Philippians, which we had nicknamed the "happy chapter."

By the end of seven months, both mom and I had survived the strain. Some days we even smiled more than we cried. We had made it, depending on each other and on God, and it gave us closeness that in some way softened the blow of what we had lost.

I've heard Jesse Jackson, the black preacher from Chicago, tell poor black people, "Nobody's gonna help us but *us*." That was true in our family. The outside people we had tried to lean on just couldn't understand what we were going through. We had only each other—and God—to rely on.

I received a better idea of what a family is supposed to be in those few months than I had ever gotten while our family was living together. I got the picture by trying to replace what was missing from my family. I first tried all my friends. I would hang around them, visit their homes, try to replace that vast sense of loneliness by letting their families rub off on me. It wouldn't work. Always my friends let me down. If we would disagree or have a minor quarrel, I would suddenly be shut out, unwelcome. I couldn't build trust in a relationship that could be cut off at any moment. I would press too hard, try to get too close to people, and they would back off.

Desperate, I started attending every church I could think of. I found that the youth groups, especially, were cliquish. Each one had its own set of standards of what kind of person it would let inside. Because I was from a lower-class background, I was excluded from many of them. Soon I knew that I would never find a replacment for family there.

I began to see that a family was a place in which you *belonged* above all else. You could run away, be put in jail, cut off contact with your family, but you would still belong. Those people carried your name. In some strange way you were linked together with them with cords that could never be cut. And that's why I felt so hurt about my dad—I was linked with him, and yet he'd walked out on us. He had tried to cut those cords, and pretend we no longer existed.

I am still learning to trust other people. After being hurt so badly with my dad, who knew everything about me and still rejected me by leaving, it's hard to open up to anyone else. Maybe God can give me the strength for that too. I've learned how important a family is by seeing my own family shattered. Our security and trust splintered overnight. We'll never restore all that was broken.

I hear kids at school run down their families, and I can't help remembering how I used to cut down my own family. Until one day when there was nothing left to cut down. . . . ■

The Wall Comes Down

by Anne Frewin

■ In a few weeks I'll be going home for Christmas. It will be the first time in more than three years that I've seen my family. Looking back to other Christmases, the ones I spent alone, it seems this Christmas will be special for me, in a way none of the others were. This year "the wall" comes down.

Resentment is a wall. It's a living barrier that grows up between people. It forces mistrust, bitterness, and misunderstanding between us. It cuts us off. It tears us apart.

Resentment is a wall between people. You can only dismantle your side

I've read where sometimes, when countries are at war, battle lines are relaxed for Christmas; combat ceases for a few hours so the soldiers can celebrate. Well, not in my family. A wall of resentment had grown up that even Christmas couldn't penetrate.

Oh, there were Christmas celebrations and festivities as usual, only I was not invited to be a part of them. I was absent because, for my parents, I did not exist. I was no longer their daughter; I had no place in their home.

The touchy situation at home had reached the breaking point my last year in high school. I decided only suicide or running away could solve my problems. I was sick and tired of not being understood. The constant grating on each other, the clashing tempers and bitterness were just too much. So, one bright day I packed up a few belongings and walked out.

I didn't go far; I moved in with a lady I had done some babysitting for. "Anytime you need a place to stay, Annie . . ." she'd told me. I took her up on her offer. I desperately needed a place to live where I

Image/Marcia Hunt

could get myself together and decide what I was going to do with myself. I knew she would just let me be.

I was comfortable living with Mrs. Benson. I took care of her two little boys while she worked during the day. And she helped me find myself, building my ruined self-confidence. I had gained more than fifty pounds in the past year living at home; she helped me pick out clothes that were flattering and somewhat stylish so I wouldn't have to wear the same old smock tops. With her influence I began losing weight and feeling better about myself.

I got a chance to think, too. I thought about my family, trying to discover what had gone wrong. We had always been close, maybe too close. I had three other sisters and we had never had many friends outside our close little circle. We never visited other girls or had people over to our house. My parents were strict traditionalists where our family was concerned—"the family that plays together, stays together."

In spite of all that closeness, it was hard to talk about the things that mattered to me. It was as if we were a very friendly group of strangers. We never spoke about our feelings or struggles. We never mentioned our fears or the problems that were bothering us. Love was just a word; in my family you didn't demonstrate it.

The wall grew taller, and soon I couldn't communicate with anyone—even my mother was at a loss to help me understand what was happening. Often out of utter frustration I would let my temper get the best of me, usually over foolish, childish things that meant nothing. For example, one Sunday afternoon my parents wanted me to go with them for a visit to my grandmother's. For some reason I decided I didn't wish to go. They insisted, and in moments I had whipped up a tremendous tantrum over the incident. I screamed and cried and carried on. Finally they left me, utterly shocked and disgusted over my irrational behavior. After they had gone I cried because I didn't want to be left alone. I needed something or someone to tell me what was going on inside me. No one could.

Those kinds of scenes, repeated again and again, made life unbearable. Bitter fights, usually over completely illogical disputes, lasted for days. There were constant run-ins with my folks over all the rules they set down, rules I had always accepted but now found hard to live with. Because of me, our home became a battleground

THE TROUBLE WITH PARENTS

full of turmoil and torment. I gradually became an outsider in my own family.

I knew I was on a collision course with a nervous breakdown. I was no longer able to hold up my end of simple, normal relationships. I had become afraid of myself; I no longer knew when I was going to fly off the handle at someone. Everywhere I turned I caused pain—and I couldn't help it. That's when I moved out.

I had been living with Mrs. Benson for about seven months when I got some bad news about a guy I had known in high school. He had been driving too fast and lost control of his car, smashing it up at a railroad crossing. He was critically injured. That upset me and I didn't know what to do. I came home and told Mrs. Benson how worried I was. She said. "Let's pray about it and ask the Lord to take care of your friend." I agreed, but Mrs. Benson did all the praying; I couldn't utter a word. I felt hollow inside. Even though I thought I was a devout Catholic, like my family, I knew nothing about Jesus. Mrs. Benson obviously was very close to Him, and I wondered about that. I knew I didn't have any right to pray to Him like she did. Why? It bothered me the rest of the evening; I went to bed troubled over it.

As I lay in bed in the darkness, a thought came to me. *Why not ask Christ into my life? If He was with me, in me, I would have a right to pray to Him any time, about anything I wanted to. I wouldn't feel hollow anymore.* I didn't know exactly what to do or how to do it, but I just closed my eyes where I lay and asked Jesus to come into my life, to make me the person He wanted me to be. Immediately I felt better. Nothing unusual had happened, but I felt different somehow. I thought I should tell someone what I had done. I went downstairs in my nightgown and woke Mrs. Benson and told her. She just smiled and hugged me. She was very happy; she said it was what she had been wanting for me all along.

A month passed. Thanksgiving was approaching and I was helping Mrs. Benson with arrangements for a turkey dinner. The phone rang and I picked it up, nearly dropping it when I found out it was my mother. She told me the family was getting together for Thanksgiving and she asked me to come home. She was asking me to come home to stay. I was overjoyed.

I shouldn't have been. Almost from the moment I walked in the door I could sense that nothing had changed. They were still the same parents I had always known, and as far as they were concerned, I was still the same, too. I set out at once to prove that I had changed. Christ had changed me.

Looking back on it now I can see it was a big mistake trying to prove something to them—that Christ was in my life and in me—something which should have been obvious in the way I lived. I never missed a chance to tell them about Jesus. I told them He was the answer; I told them of the happiness I had now. They would listen to me go on and on, trying to convert them. But, because I was still such a new Christian with so many problems, they couldn't understand. I wasn't able to show the answer in my life. Soon I was right back to the old frustration. Tensions were building once again.

My parents were frustrated, too. I had been home only a little while when they realized how much more peaceful things had been while I was away. One morning my father called me into the living room. It was quiet in the house; mother was away on some errand. He was sitting in his usual place, a green, overstuffed easy chair. It was plain that we had both reached a stalemate. "Anne," he said, quietly, "It's not that we don't love you. . . ." He was speaking slowly, deliberately, trying not to let any emotion crack through. "But your mother and I have talked it over and we feel it would be best for all if you would find a place of your own."

I must have known that was coming. Somewhere deep in the back of my mind I guess I expected it, which is why it didn't shock me. I just remember feeling very cold. Though the familiar room was filled with morning light, it seemed to go gray and unfriendly.

"Okay, I'll go," I told him. And then we just sat there for a little while longer. Neither of us spoke, but I think we were both quite relieved. I looked through the newspaper for an apartment and it wasn't long before I found one to suit me. The next Monday morning my father loaded up my things and drove me across town to my new place. He helped me with my things and we said a cold good-by on the sidewalk outside the building. I watched him drive away and felt very small and alone.

I soon got a job, made new friends—Christian kids my own age—and began learning about life on my own. Three years have gone by and I've learned a lot about myself. My friends have loved and reinforced me, helping me find God's way for my life. I could never have made it without their help and God's.

THE TROUBLE WITH PARENTS

A week ago I got a letter in the morning mail. It was from my mother. She and dad are inviting me home for Christmas. I can stay in my old room if I want to, and things will be like they used to be, she says. Well, things won't be like they used to be—they never are. I've grown and matured. I've learned to love my parents for what they are and not hate them for what they aren't.

Hopefully, I've shed most of my self-centeredness and I've developed patience in doing things God's way. I'm going to show them in tangible ways that I appreciate them, such as spending some time with my mother alone. I'm keeping my eyes open for opportunities to show my respect for them; I'll go along with my father's rules and help with the chores around the house. I'm not going home to change my parents; I'm going home to love them and let them love me. I want this Christmas to be the warmest ever. This Christmas the wall comes down. ■

Shelter

by Tim Stafford

■ His parents had never hidden their quarrels. Rob sat in the kitchen alone, with all the lights out in the dark afternoon, and thought of one fight in particular. It had happened years ago, in their old house. He could still see his mother lying stretched on the floor, crying softly amid worn Oriental rugs and faded furniture.

No one had hit her; she had lain down herself after sharp words with his father, who sat in a chair helplessly reading the paper. It was Sunday afternoon. Hearing her crying, Rob had approached her and tried to say something comforting. The words were long since lost in his memory, but the cautious attempt to soothe still came through the intonation, which he remembered. His mother

Sometimes you can't make pain go away, or make wrong things right. You can still survive, and you can still love

raised her head just enough to snap some words at him, and he retreated, bewildered. Later his father said softly, in a male-to-male way, "You can't talk to women when they're upset, Rob. You have to leave them alone until they're over it."

Right now Rob was breaking bread into chunks, smearing each with butter and then dipping it in the sugar bowl. His mother hated the habit, because it left crumbs everywhere. Already they were spreading across the dark walnut table. But Rob didn't care. He was thinking about that incident. It stood in his memory as clearly as an old film, yet he had never given it much significance, never taken it for a signal that his family was disintegrating. Yet this afternoon his father had asked him, in a way that would not allow a "no," to go for a drive. He then told Rob that he and his mother were going to get a divorce. They would tell the rest of the kids that night. He wanted Rob to know first because he was the oldest, and could help to keep things calm.

Rob had said nothing, and his father had looked over at him, trying to see what he was thinking. "Don't think we hate each other," he continued. "Rob, we don't. But we seem to endlessly make each other miserable. I don't know why. We've tried to make it work." Then he said, in a burst beyond the calmness he'd put on, "Rob, I hate doing this to you."

Rob had been stunned by the news: his mind had seemed to run circles around the words, finding no hanging phrase to grasp and understand. The explanation "we make each other miserable" had seemed enough; now, as he broke the bread and slathered butter over it, it made no sense at all. Happiness was not a miracle, or an accident, was it? If they were miserable now, what made it that way? They must have been happy together at some time. But search his mind as he could Rob could find no image of pure joy between them. They had always seemed very different—"You can't talk to women. . . ." He loved his father—loved him for the sloppy clothes his mother fought against, for the compliance with which he accepted the decisions his mother insisted on and yet somehow ignored them or found a way around.

Rob took a new slice of bread from the wrapper, and remembered that if he were very careful, he could pull it exactly in half, as straight as if he had creased it first. He tried it—it worked. He got another slice and pulled it apart too, in even halves—then a third and a fourth piece, each one splitting down the middle. Then he laughed. The table was covered with bread he would never eat. He wanted to tear more, but thought that he was acting silly.

His mother came in with groceries fifteen minutes later, and he still sat with the scattered bread in front of him. His first reaction was to cover it, sure that she'd nag at the waste and the mess. But when she looked and said nothing, dumping the grocery sack on the sideboard, he realized that she knew his father had told him.

"Sorry about the bread," he said. "I was trying to tear it straight."

She didn't seem to hear. "Where did your father go?"

"He didn't say."

She stared at him for a moment, as though she had forgotten

THE TROUBLE WITH PARENTS

what she was going to say. "He never does," she said finally. "Did he talk to you, Rob?"

Lies entered his mind. "About what?" he could say. How would she handle that? But all he said was, "Yes." He said it without looking at her.

"Well, then you know," she said, faintly relieved. "You can help us tonight. It might be hard for Chrissie and Reggie to understand, Rob. It might frighten them."

He left his back to her like a wall. To punish her, to frighten her, he said nothing. But he was thinking, *And why should I understand? And why should I help you cover up?*

Eventually he turned and looked at her. She showed no emotion. Her short, black hair was perfectly in place. She looked like all the other mothers. "Are there any more groceries outside?" he asked, and without waiting for an answer went to get them.

When he called Reggie and Chrissie that night they were watching "Chico and the Man" and didn't want to come. He told them they had to, and enjoyed saying it. If he suffered they would have to suffer too. Reggie was thirteen, Chrissie, ten. Reggie had long, floppy brown hair that made him look too old. He reached out his foot and kicked the off switch; the TV went blank. "Don't kick that," Rob said.

"Why not?"

"Mom says you'll break something. You know that."

"That's how dad does it."

In the living room his father had built a fire, and both parents sat in front of it, close together. The three kids sat at the end of the room. Reggie whined, "How long is this going to take?"

"Never mind how long," his father said. "Come sit down here." His face looked the color of the ashes you found in the morning— dead. All afternoon Rob had been angry but now he felt afraid. He glanced at his mother, thinking that she would have dressed for the occasion. But she wore her kitchen apron, as though she'd been interrupted in the middle of something more important.

Chrissie moved closer: she always obeyed. Reggie stayed where he was; perhaps he sensed what was coming. Their father reached out and took their mother's hand, held it for a moment and then began.

"I'm going to be moving to another house," he said. "We've

decided—your mother and I—that it's better that way. I kind of hope we'll all end up happier. You kids, too. I won't be very far away, and you'll still see me all the time. I just won't live here, and you'll have to listen to what your mom says."

Reggie took it calmly. He asked, "Whose house are you gonna live in?"

His father still looked gray. "I don't know. Nobody's. It will be my house. An apartment, actually, down near the train station."

"Like those high-rise ones?"

"No, but it's near there."

"Aw, I wish it were one of those high-rise ones. You can see for fifty miles from the top of one of those."

His mother tried to smile. No one spoke. Then Reggie said, "Is that all? Can we go watch TV?"

His father glanced at his mother, asking, "Is that all you want them to know?" She said, "Daddy's leaving tomorrow. If you want to ask anything you ought to ask it now."

Chrissie started to cry, and for a moment no one said anything. Rob's mother moved over, picked her up, and held her chubby body. Chrissie kept crying. "What is it, Chrissie?" her mother asked. "Why are you crying? There's nothing to cry about. Daddy will still be near."

"Are you gonna be divorced?" Chrissie asked. One of her friends was going through the same thing.

His mother took it in stride; Rob watched her face for any sign of grief. "Daddy and mommy won't be married to each other any more. But we won't fight like Arlene's parents. We like each other very much, and we will always be friends. So you won't have to worry."

But Rob wanted them to fight. He wanted to scream at them. In a voice as nasty as he could make it he asked, "If you still like each other so well, what do you want to get divorced for?"

His parents looked at each other again, asking. Then his mother said, "Reggie, you and Chrissie can go watch TV now if you want, if you don't have any more questions." Reggie got up, but lingered near the door. Chrissie stayed in her arms. Rob's mother said to him, "You can be good friends and still not want to be married to each other. Both of us have good friends that we aren't in love with."

"But you *did* get married. Weren't you ever in love then? What's changed now?"

His father intervened, appealing with his eyes for Rob to be gentler. Rob felt the water begin to swim in his own eyes, and he felt angry and bitter at himself for being so weak, especially in front of his father. "Rob," his father said, "many things change. It's almost twenty years ago that we got married. We're not saying it was a mistake. We're saying it would be a mistake to go on."

"But whose fault is it?" Rob demanded. He was crying now. "It doesn't just happen, does it? If you stopped loving each other, then someone must have made that happen. Why won't you tell me?"

His father faltered, and Rob saw him begin to cry. It was the first time he had ever seen it. His father lowered his big, shaggy head into his hands and said nothing.

"Rob, you don't have to shout," his mother said.

"I'm not shouting!"

"You're frightening Chrissie. Please help us, as we asked."

He put his own head down and listened. "Rob," she said, "it doesn't have to be anyone's fault. When two people fall apart you usually can't lay the blame on one person's head more than the other. And it doesn't do any good."

Rob said nothing now. He had never lost control this much: he kept his head down, sobbing, embarrassed and afraid, and thinking perversely of what he would tell kids at school. He couldn't stand to think of their sympathy. Then his father came and put his arms around him and for the first time in Rob's seventeen years, they cried together.

He was sure afterward that his mother was to blame. Why hadn't she cried? Why wouldn't she let the real cause of the split come out?

When he came home from school the next day his father was gone, and Rob ate supper in a mask of silence. He refused to look at his mother; when she looked at him he looked away. *The perfect suburban mother,* he was thinking. Neat and organized, active and cold. She wanted things to look right; she didn't care about whether they really *were* right. When you cut to the heart of her nice-looking things, what spilled out? Little balls of Styrofoam, handy as a filler material.

He knew he was unfair to her: he loved her; but it was easier to be angry, and to multiply examples of the differences between his parents. His hapless, lovable father followed dutifully behind her to fancy dinners given by artistic people he didn't like; his mother bought his father clothes that fit perfectly and had the right kind of collars; his father claimed quietly that he felt like a circus animal and went back to wearing the baggy pants he felt comfortable in; his father loved hot-dog stands and grease-soaked joints for lunch when they traveled, and his mother talked uneasily about the "atmosphere" of the place, while sitting poised, as though she might catch a disease if she put her weight on anything. Yes, it was easy to multiply examples, and he found himself shouting at his mother in his thoughts, though consciously he tried to be fair, and certainly said nothing to transmit his feeling to Reggie and Chrissie.

Apart from his own sullenness, things went on annoyingly smoothly; his father was gone as if on a selling trip, unmissed. Once that week he stopped in, not to see them, but to retrieve some extra clothes. Rob's mother stayed in the den watching TV. Though Rob longed to tell his father how much he loved him and was on his side, he only managed to be shyly friendly. "Come down and see me after school," his father said as he left. "Anytime."

No one at school seemed to know, which pressed Rob's thoughts more into himself. He could see his friends in an odd, new way; he watched their faces as they talked, and heard how stupid the conversations were. Their voices seemed to come from a speaker turned up too loud, distorted. Their faces looked like a movie—the sound disembodied. He didn't want to talk to them; he thought all the time about his parents, and only when he buried himself in the booming mechanical frenzy of basketball after school did he forget. He thought about what his father had said: "Come see me. Anytime." If he requested it, they might let his father have custody of him. That would be unfair to his mother, to Reggie, and Chrissie, but it would serve her right. He would make her sorry.

Tuesday night, a week and a half after he heard the news, he walked home alone from basketball. It was already dark, and the cars swishing past had the sound and look of the machine: the two unwearying eyes, and the quiet white whirring that trailed off at the end. Leafless trees clutched at the purplish sky; from the houses he passed came yellow light and warm kitchen smells, but he didn't want to go home. He decided, in a second, to go see his father.

It was cold, but the walk wasn't far. He wondered what his father would say, and what they could talk about; having decided to go see him he felt jumpy. He hoped they could talk, glumly and secretly, of failure and the unfairness of women, and he and his father would be close together again. Rob was weary of working against his mother; he wanted a renewed sense that his father was right, and that it was their struggle, together. It was the sort of feeling he had when the basketball team won, and he saw Ricky Crosby in class. Everyone else might know they had won, but no one knew it as they did.

He had driven by the apartment before. It was a three-story brick building with a drugstore next door; it was hard to guess what things looked like inside. He found his father's name and pressed the buzzer, then waited, shivering slightly in the cold tile hallway lit only by the street light outside. For a moment he was afraid his father was gone, but then a speaker clicked, and he heard a metallic voice asking who it was. "It's me, dad, Rob."

There was a brief pause, then another click, and his father said, "All right. Come on up." A buzzer released the door, and he walked slowly up to the second floor. His father stood with the door open, in his socks, smiling roundly. His hair was thrown in tufts around his head, messier than usual. "I'm glad you came, Rob. Come on in."

Feeling shy, he sat across the room from his father. The furniture did not fit: it was wicker with bright, coarse-woven material. Someone else, not his father, had chosen it.

"How's your mom?" his father asked, slumped in a chair.

"She's okay, I guess."

"Reggie? Chrissie?"

"I don't think they know what's happened, dad." He said it meaning to be comrades, but his father turned away. "They just act like you're on a business trip," he added.

"Yeah," his father said. "They'll probably only realize it in a few more weeks, I guess."

His father's face looked numb and distracted, as though Rob had interrupted him in his thoughts. He made no effort to open himself. Rob asked, "What were you doing?"

"Looking at the paper. You know that's what I always do after work."

"And mom always gets mad because you throw it all over the room. 'Like living with a hamster,' she says." He tried to grin.

"Oh, gee, your mother," his father said, and rubbed his eyes.

SHELTER

77

"She's really something." Then he looked up sharply. "You help her out with Reggie."

He stood up and walked across the room. "You want anything to eat? No? What brought you here, Rob? Did you want to talk to me about something?"

"No, not really. You said to come by."

"Oh, yeah. Sure, that's good. I wondered if you had something particular in mind."

Rob chanced it: fought the reluctance to talk to his father face-to-face. "Just wanted to say," and the words came out like something that burns, "that I *am* on your side, dad. I mean, I don't blame you."

His father looked blank; again it was as though his thoughts had been interrupted. "You don't blame me? Funny, I blame myself. Leaving you kids.

"Look," his father continued, still pacing absent-mindedly, "Rob, I don't know how to tell you. Your mother and I just don't see eye-to-eye. But you mind her. She's right about a lot of those things."

There was quiet while his father looked at him. "Dad," Rob said, "I don't want to mind her. Not after seeing her nag you out. I don't want to live there."

His father seemed to dodge the question. He changed the subject to baseball, though Rob, once having brought up the possibility of leaving home, wanted to butt in and raise it again. But he was caught up in the shambling, anarchic spirit his father generated, laughing at a story he had heard before about a shortstop named Zacharias who tried to steal the ball after each game. His father punctuated the story with karate-like jabs of his stiff-fingered hands. His eyes gleamed.

Rob butted in. "I'm just thinking that in only a year I'll be gone to college. One year more away won't matter to Reggie and Chrissie either way."

His father seemed not to hear. "You know I used to take your mother to games in Los Angeles, back when they first moved out from Brooklyn. She never liked it, but on the other hand she wouldn't stay home. We used to sit in the bleachers, and they had these incredible splinters your mother was always snagging her stockings on. She hated it. You can imagine.

"Anyway, one time I noticed she was really unhappy. I didn't

THE TROUBLE WITH PARENTS

think about it, you know. I just thought she was displeased about being at a baseball game. Then I was buying a hot dog, and the guy reached across her and kind of bumped her. Well, she really snapped at him. 'Don't you have any manners?' So he said, 'What's the matter, lady? You got a splinter in your girdle?' And then your mother started turning red. She turned as red as a beet, and I just started laughing and couldn't quit. It was true. A big splinter about as long as your finger. We went right home. Oh, you should have seen her!" Rob laughed hilariously and clapped his hands. "That was her last baseball game. She won't even watch it on TV now."

Then Rob stopped laughing and said plainly, "Dad, will you listen? I want to live with you. I don't want to go home. Okay?"

His father turned slowly grave. He stuttered before saying in a low voice, "I don't think that's too good an idea, Rob. I would love to have you, but it wouldn't work."

"I *hate* her."

"No, you can't. You won't for long. It's not her fault."

Rob felt distance growing between them. "I don't care," he said. "Why can't I live here? Why?" His voice broke, and he hated his little-boy tone.

Slowly his father spoke, "Well, Rob, I'm hoping to remarry. It'll be a while before I can. Maybe then. But you'll be away at college, so it won't matter. Until then it wouldn't work." His father's voice was quiet, his face shut.

Then the new thoughts began flooding Rob's mind. He hesitated before asking. "You already know who you're going to marry?"

His father nodded, looking away.

"Oh, wow," was all he said. Things looked different; he sat thinking, and his father's bumbling casual appearance became in his mind a pose and betrayal. He felt like he ought to leave. He felt he did not belong there.

Standing up, he said, "Dad, I'm going to go." Not waiting for an answer he walked out, then clattered down the stairs.

His father caught him at the bottom. Rob didn't want to turn to him, but he seized Rob's shoulder and held it so tight it hurt. He had huge hands. There were tear streaks down his face, and they reflected the street lights outside. "Rob," he said. "I'm sorry. Why don't you stay the night? I'll call your mother."

But Rob said nothing; he was holding himself up firm, away from his father. So it was his father's cover-up too; perhaps mostly his. Rob said the worst thing he could think of: "I wouldn't want to be in her way."

"What?"

"Whatever her name is—your friend." Then he broke loose and ran for a block until he knew his father was not following. He turned and looked for him, but there was no one visible, and the street was dark, mottled only with the aura where street lights lit the ground. He was alone, and he knew that now he could not be on anyone's side; not his mother's or his father's. There was no right side; it was all simply broken. Could he ever love his father again? He wondered the same about his mother. He wondered if he would ever have a whole heart again for anyone.

But by the time he reached his home the exercise of walking had broken down the fierceness of his rage. He would survive, he thought, though his family would never again seem like a safe place to run to.

Standing outside the house, ashamed to go in with his face stained, he saw the light come on in the kitchen. Reggie's head moved across the lighted rectangle; his mouth was moving though no words penetrated the glass. Rob thought of his father, and felt a stab of pity for him. He wondered if his father would ever walk here at night and watch to see his, Rob's face in the window, and yet not be able to come in and talk.

And then he thought of his mother, and realized how tired she must feel—tired, and perhaps rejected. But she was strong, too strong, if that was possible. Perhaps she hadn't cried because she thought she could not afford to spend the tears. He pictured her made-up face and wondered if it masked over hurt, or worry, or fear. Then he felt, inside, a movement, like love returning. He went inside. ∎

THE TROUBLE WITH PARENTS

Growing Up Normal

■ My family's problems started with my father. He was (and is) a doctor, a respected citizen of our small New England town. I remember coming home one day and finding he wasn't there. My mother was acting very nervous and tense and my brother asked her where dad was. She said, "He's sick. He's at the hospital."

His sickness, we found out, was the kind you give yourself. He was addicted to drugs and had been for a long time. It's not so unusual a phenomenon as you might think; some say ten percent of all doctors are addicted, prescribing for themselves. **You can't live two lives—one with God and the other with your family**

They're very good at disguising it. My own father certainly was, and that's why no one had suspected it for so long. We kids had

by Linda Shaffer

wondered if something was wrong, for you can't hide all the symptoms all the time. Sometimes it would be hard for him to get up out of his chair. He often looked abnormally tired.

Dad was gone for six months. Our income disappeared, and suddenly, instead of living on a more-than-comfortable doctor's income, we were scraping for every penny. That, combined with the confusion and embarrassment when people found out about dad, made the most miserable six months I had ever spent. You read about families pulling together when things get hard, but that didn't happen to us. There didn't seem to be any love in our family at all. It was constant fighting and arguing.

When my father came home we thought things would improve, but a bitterness stayed that we couldn't shake. His license had been restricted, so we still had very little money. He and my mother were constantly battling, trying to use me and my brothers and sisters against each other. It was imposssible not to take sides sometimes, and when you did, it turned out worse. My father had always gambled, and now with money scarce, that took on drastic implications. Sometimes he would disappear for a few days and we would assume he'd gone to Las Vegas again. We never asked: it would only start a fight. The drugs didn't stop either, though he was more careful. He drank more.

More than anything I longed to just be normal, to live a quiet life with plenty of peace and a lot less worry. But I had no idea where or how that was possible.

Then a girl friend from school began to invite me over to her house. I found a completely different world. Her home was as peaceful as a garden, an incredible contrast to the screaming and fighting that were the continual background music in ours. Her parents were so loving, and they seemed to actually *trust* her.

For a long time I didn't understand where their love came from. Gradually I understood that it came from God, because they were Christians. I doubt anyone was ever more open to God's love than I was then. I had always wanted to understand how I could know Him personally. Ellen's family did, and I was eager to learn. Within a few months of my first visit, I had asked Jesus to enter my life.

Love flooded over me. I had never felt it before, never dreamed it could be so intense or so beautiful. I went to all kinds of meetings where Christians my age were together. People there cared about me. They would listen to me. No one knew what my family was like, nor did they care to pry into it. I kept it a secret, feeling very glad to be free of it, finding a new beginning in life. No one knew about my father's addiction or my mother's paranoia (in the supermarket she was sure everyone was looking at her, laughing at her).

Gradually I drove myself into a cycle of guilty failure at home. I didn't tell my family about Christ. I kept searching for some dramatic time when I would tell them everything. The idea of gradually sharing Jesus' love didn't occur to me. I felt wretched. All the things that we were told at church about loving our parents seemed impossible.

That tension continued all the way through high school. Away from home I was free and happy, at least superficially. At home I was anxious, tense, and angry. I became bitter, the source of fights.

I wanted my Christian friends to understand my home situation, but I felt they could not. I wanted my family to understand the Christian love I had found, but I felt they couldn't. My two worlds stayed apart.

Then a wonderful thing happened. I graduated from high school and went away to college.

I arrived at school in the fall. It was a big state university, easy to get lost in. The freedom I found overwhelmed me. There was so much to do, so many people to meet. My family? Who were they? I felt I had worried about them too long, and it hadn't done any good. During that year my parents separated and began proceedings for a divorce. I didn't know whether to feel good or bad. I was just glad to be away—free.

I stopped worrying about my family. I only thought about them while home on vacation, and then my concern was how to survive until I got back to school. In the fall of my sophomore year I heard that my father had gone off drugs and was cleaning himself up. He had vowed to do that before, of course, but this time he was supposed to be really changing. Was it possible?

I didn't know, and I didn't think much about it. I had gotten so used to tragedy, I didn't know what to do with hope, especially hope that just came out of the blue. *Maybe,* I remember thinking, *things are going to work out without me, God, without anyone.* It was a vaguely cheerful thought.

That semester I carried a terrible course load. I kept to myself. My roommate was a strong Christian, but I wouldn't let myself get too close to her. I worked hard at my classes, and by finals felt very tired. I caught a cold but ignored it. I stayed up all night before one final. The next day I was so sick I couldn't even take the test. Yet I kept on studying, trying frantically to finish.

I never made it. When I finally went to see a doctor, he told me I was a fool for not coming sooner and put me in the health center. I had to cancel several finals, but by that time I didn't care. After several wretched days in the health center, I took a long, dreary train ride home, running a fever of 104°.

For once the atmosphere at home didn't matter. I stayed in bed nearly the whole time, exhausted and feverish. Only near the end of the "vacation" did I begin to feel better, and even then I was weak. I got my grades and found that I had failed a course. It was the first time that had happened, and I felt terrible.

Then came registration: the lines and faces back again. I saw a few friends and had to tell them the story of what had happened to my finals. I went to register, and met my younger brother outside; alphabetically we were together. We waded through the line, got our courses and cards and found ourselves outside again. Something was bothering him, I could tell. Streams of people were walking by us; it was bitterly cold. Then he told me, very quickly and matter-of-factly, what had happened to my dad. He was under arrest, Jim said, for killing a man. There had been a fight in a bar, some shots were fired, and a man had been killed. The gun they found was in my dad's name. They had searched for him for two days before he gave himself up. The story was in all the local papers.

My brother left immediately—coldly, I thought at the time, though later I realized it hurt him too much to talk. And there I was, in the middle of streams of people, standing in the falling snow, alone. I began to cry, shaking. It hurt more than I would ever have imagined. I could hardly stand it, it hurt so bad.

There is something about parents. No matter how hard you push them away, you can't get detached. You are stuck with them, good or bad. I thought I was rid of my family; I thought I had them tucked away into my past. But when I heard that news, nothing else seemed to matter. I felt alone in a way I had never felt before. There was no one—no one at all—who cared for me or my family.

Then, suddenly, there was someone. There were 36,000 students on the campus, and the only one who could have helped me suddenly appeared: my roommate. One moment I was standing alone on the steps, crying, and the next she was holding my arms, asking what was the matter. Her boyfriend stood questioningly in the background. I sobbed out my story. She hugged me, and then they took me home.

For the next week I didn't do much. I lay on my bed a lot, and I cried and cried and cried. I cried not merely for my father, I cried for myself. I cried for my life. When I thought of how, all down the threads of my life, God had helped me and sheltered me, and when I thought of the way I rewarded Him . . . I cried.

I cried for things I couldn't name: for a million fights fought in our home, for the hatred and bitterness toward God and my own family, for my own sense of guilt. I cried for my mother and my brothers and my sister, and of course for my father. But most of all, I cried for myself.

Gradually I came to myself. I knew that things couldn't stay the same. There had to be a radical change. My two worlds had to come together, not because of guilt, or fear, but because of love.

My roommate helped. We talked, and she encouraged me. Best of all, for the first time I took a real interest in the Christians who met to pray and study the Bible together.

Finally the semester ended, and I went home.

I found that much was the same. I guess I had hoped for a bombshell. It didn't hit. There were still fights, and I was still sometimes the cause of them. But one thing had changed: I was committed to love. Before I had wanted to witness for a variety of reasons: my own guilt feelings, my desire to have the "right" kind of family, my sense of duty. Now I had given my whole life—not half of it—to Christ.

I didn't say much. I talked to my little sister, who had become a Christian recently. Together we tried to show love to our family. My mother would never listen to us: there was always mockery when Christianity came up. So we lived on simple things, letting our actions and love speak for themselves. And we continue to do so. Sometimes God had come up in the way we talked, often enough so that we are called the family "Jesus freaks." The mockery for that has decreased. Love has begun to conquer.

I find that my whole sense of the pace of things has changed. Before, I wanted God to change my family in a week, or a month at the most. Of course, I knew He could do that. But now I am happy for the smallest things: for the understanding we are growing into.

We are far behind schedule. I have so much to learn about love. I feel as though, with my mother, I'm at the level of a twelve-year-old. A recent shopping excursion brought that home to me. While we were driving to the shopping center she began, very seriously, to talk to me about the evils of smoking. I looked up to see whether she was serious. Could it be she was completely unaware that I had grown too old for that kind of mother-daughter lecture? "Mother," I wanted to say, "where have you been all this time?"

But then I thought, *Linda, where have you been all this time?* And so I kept quiet, and listened. If you want to bring your worlds together, sometimes you have to start at the zero point. ∎

If You Can'

Trust Your Mother by Karen Kerr

■ My mother betrayed me. I couldn't get that thought out of my mind. I had always trusted and confided in her. We were close friends and I told her everything. Like the first time a boy kissed me: the kiss lasted thirty seconds and frightened me stiff. But I could talk over anything with my mother and she would calm me down and love me.

No more. I was convinced I could never trust her again. The signs started cropping up on a six-month vacation to Mexico with mother and my three younger sisters. My parents had always fought, but at the time I

Her parents split and left her alone with bitterness

didn't suspect anything like a "separation" was going on. In Mexico, my mother met a young, long-haired man named Jeff. Twelve years younger than mother, he lived in a trailer, and we first thought she was just relieved to find a friendly American in Mexico. But nothing stayed the same after that trip.

Dad sensed the storm brewing soonest, probably because he was part of the problem. He became more distant, taking long business trips and not calling us like he used to. At home, he and mother picked at each other, igniting arguments from trivialities such as who would dry the dishes, or what to do on a weekend night.

Wallowitch

89

My sisters and I were confused and hurt. Naturally at first I depended more on my mother, and she comforted me. She would hold me close and tell me there was no real problem in the family . . . there would be no divorce. Our family was too precious to rot apart like old fruit. And for awhile I believed her. Perhaps she believed it, too . . . for awhile.

But divorce proceedings came quickly. Divorce—my mother had assured me innumerable times there would be no divorce. Suddenly, there it was. Oh, sure, the evidence had been there all the time. For weeks my parents had argued late into the night while I crouched by the crack in their door listening, my stomach knotted in confusion and fear. Sometimes the arguments were about me, and I wanted to rush in shrieking, but I sat alone with my tears. Still, I was blind to reality.

Then divorce proceedings started. I could not accept it. I began to hate mother; she had broken my illusions.

I felt the ache of a fractured world the first thing when I awoke every morning. It followed me through classes in school all day. I lingered at school, joining clubs that met in the afternoon so I could avoid home. Often I would go to friends' homes rather than my own, wanting mother to suffer. When I did go home, I would lie awake for hours, remembering past nights when mother would talk me to sleep.

Gradually I became aloof and lonely. At school, I couldn't face the pressure of competition. Everyone seemed to exploit his or her own unique quality. The blonde cheerleaders with their Breck-clean hair and upturned noses. The dandruffy chemistry whizzes who played chess on note cards during class. The swaggering greasers and mod dressers. None of those things seemed important—nothing did.

I often felt I was in a trance: my body going through the motions while leaving my mind back at home, ringing with mother and dad's angry shouts. After a time, I couldn't put up the front I needed every day to look normal. I knew I had to find some support to fill the vacuum where my mother had been. But I didn't think anyone could understand my hurt.

Drugs helped some, by shielding me from the world with a glazed-over mask. Nothing mattered as much when I was on drugs.

Then Jeff—the guy from Mexico—came to Houston. Mother perked up, brighter and more cheery than I had seen her in years.

She spent extra time in front of the mirror, fixing her hair and face. She seemed to be in love. The truth cut me like a knife. Jeff was cordial, tried to befriend my sisters and me, but I was repulsed. He would ask one of my sisters to do something, or set a rule about phone calls or dating, and I would fly into a rage, slamming doors and cursing him.

The fantasies came at night, I don't know whether from the drugs or just from the smoldering hatred. But instead of crying myself to sleep, I began to fantasize what it would be like to kill people. I would visualize murdering mother and Jeff and other people I didn't like. First a face . . . then a flash of a gun . . . then blackness.

My only real source of comfort came in conversations with a biology teacher, Mike Turnage, who happened to be a Christian. One day when there weren't any students near he came up to me and told me he could see what I was going through. He also said he had an answer to my problems. I could not help but cry—the first tears I had shed in many bitter months. I had at last found a human being who cared. But I wasn't ready for his answer—Jesus Christ. I only trusted myself—and I had to cling to that.

On an especially bad night, mother finally cracked. I had baited her, scorned her, turned my sister against her, made life miserable for her—all in revenge against her for betraying me. She burst into my room, screaming incoherently, cursing and yelling something about marijuana I had stolen. She flipped on the light, and I shielded my eyes, recoiling from the brightness.

Until then my room had been the only orderly part of my life remaining. I kept it spotless, every book in place, every picture straight, every drawer closed. It was my last unspoiled haven. Mother wildly tore the room apart. She ripped sheets off the bed and swept the bookshelves clean with her arm. All my treasures and books clattered to the floor. After fifteen minutes of harangue she yelled, "Get out! Get out! Tell your father to pick you up. I don't want you in my house!"

I was cowering beside my bed, speechless and sobbing. I had never seen her out of control. I had dreamed of driving mother to something like this by torturing her, but when it happened I felt very sick and lonely. Everything had turned against me.

I stepped through the broken china animals and photo frames and mementos on the floor and ran to Kathy's room. She had locked it in fear, and I couldn't even call out to her. I could only gasp between sobs, scratching at the door for help. Kathy came, saw what happened, and ran to mother's room yelling. The haranguing began again.

Dad came that night, and I left my room for the last time. With him I became even more withdrawn, living my own life, causing a little trouble at school, but refusing deep friendships.

The conversations with Mike Turnage made me restless. God's spiritual warfare for my mind and soul had begun. It was a hard-fought battle filled with sleepless nights. I kept a personal notebook at the time, and in it I compared my spiritual battle to two great dams. On one dam were Mike and other loving Christians he had introduced me to, and on the other were my psychologist, my boyfriend and my fierce self-reliance. I wrote: "I'm standing in the middle of two great, cracked dams with torrents of water on either side. At first just a few drops of water trickled down and tickled my toes. Now there is a steady stream flowing. The water bothers me and my feet are cold, but my curiosity persists—and the water still rises. What will happen when the cracks enlarge? What will happen when both dams break and I am left drowning under the floods? Will I be strong enough to swim? I don't know."

After the school year closed, Mike suggested I visit Camp Peniel, a Christian camp in West Texas. I went, and the dams broke. For a week and a half I argued with camp counselors and staff on an intellectual level about Christianity.

Working in the camp laundry, I came in contact with many people. I could turn off most of them just by refusing to act interested. One lady was different, though. She was loving. Even though I hated all women because of my mother, she managed to crack the barriers with love. She attacked my pride, softly, yet firmly. It was this lady who attracted me to Christ. I wanted the love she lived. I knelt with her, not fully knowing what I was doing, and asked Jesus to take control of my life. It was mostly an intellectual decision . . . I didn't have many emotions left.

Two days after I accepted Christ the bottom dropped out. Mother called and said she was taking my three sisters to California to live with Jeff. On the phone I acted cool and unaffected, but inside I was boiling. As soon as she hung up I ran to a wooded area and tried to get my thoughts together.

If mother didn't really mean anything to me, why was I feeling like this? Why couldn't I blot out that void her leaving brought on? How could I love and hate her at the same time? And how did God fit into this? Those verses the lady had read me from the Bible—about all things working together for good—did they mean *anything?*

The pain stayed with me all through that summer camp. I resented mother for stealing my sisters and again betraying me. My new faith in Christ helped some, but as soon as school started I had to leave all my Christian friends at camp. Living for Christ got harder. I found myself slipping back into old habits—being a loner, taking dope—because I couldn't make it on my own. By the time school started mother had married Jeff, and the break was final. Our home would never again be together.

If I was at a standstill during this period, God was not. I began to receive letters from mother describing a church in Costa Mesa, California, named Calvary Chapel. I had heard about the church before, where every night thousands of long-haired, barefoot kids would go and worship God under a big canvas tent. Mother said the family had been attending the church regularly and had all accepted Jesus Christ as the Lord of their lives.

What should have been the most joyful news of my life I accepted with a shrug. What did I care about those who obviously cared so little about me? I tried to push the news out of my mind, even to blame them for taking up religion to relieve guilt feelings. But mother kept writing, even when I never answered. She admitted that she needed me.

For a long time I didn't see her. In that time my attitude melted from resentment to apathy. I no longer cared.

Kathy came to Texas for Christmas. She seemed more stable. She begged me to come see them, to give mother another chance, and cynically I wondered if mother had flown her to Texas just for those speeches.

I finally did go to California, over Easter vacation of my junior year in high school. The three-hour flight gave me plenty of time to reflect over the nine months since I had seen mother. I thought back to the mild surge of hope I had had at camp just after accepting Christ . . . until I had learned about mother leaving. I thought also of the trouble I had caused at school that year. Everyone knew me as "Karen, the little hippie." My grades had slipped and I had stumbled through the year with a lousy attitude.

My stomach was churning with apprehension and I could barely swallow the cardboard-tasting airline food. We flew over the flat Texas plain near dusk, and could faintly see the outline of California mountains before the sun dipped under. Lights of the Los Angeles suburbs stretched out for miles before the captain told us to fasten seat belts. All the streets were perfectly straight, with even spaces between the street lights. It looked so orderly, but inside I felt confused—and scared.

The plane touched down and I gritted my teeth and stepped out into the dry California air. Mother was at the gate, alone. She hadn't brought my sisters as a buffer as I had thought she would. We went through the standard hug and comments about the trip and stepped on the slidewalks that moved us through the airport. Mother seemed much shorter than I remembered. Also calmer, less tense.

As we drove off, conversation became easier. Nine months of separation gave us plenty to talk about. I opened up a little, mentioning how leery I was of seeing Jeff after all the fights we'd had. Mother could have seized a statement like that and lit into it. Instead, she said, "Don't worry, Karen—God will take care of it."

We met Jeff at the Christian hobby shop where he worked on leather goods. He enthusiastically showed me his work. He carved Christian symbols like the fish into leather belts and purses. I kept expecting someone to be uptight. I was ready for a quarrel like we used to have. But Jeff, mother, and my sisters all seemed relaxed, glad to see me. I was edgy at first, defensive, but even I relaxed after a while.

After three days I remembered I hadn't smoked one of the joints I'd brought with me. I pulled one out, smoked it and got a terrible headache. I flushed the rest down a toilet.

Calvary Chapel blew my mind. The people were so sincere and caring. Strangers would approach, sit on the ground next to me, and talk. They seemed genuinely interested in me. I found myself wanting to cling to the hurt and anger of my family—the revenge against mother—but it kept slipping away. I could remember what it was like, faintly, like remembering what happened in a movie. But I couldn't relive the emotions. It seemed like all those bad things must have happened to someone else. Everywhere I went with Jeff and mother I felt loved. I couldn't get away from the love.

I spent a lot of time with God on that trip. I couldn't have avoided Him if I had wanted. He was everywhere, in the people I met. I prayed and studied His Word, asking for healing and forgiveness. He healed me to the point where I could see how foolish and unfair I had been, and I even discussed it with Jeff and mother.

I stayed in California a few weeks; that was all it took to heal the past. There, God gave me the gift of forgetting. I would look at Jeff and see, not a disgusting kid who'd stolen my sisters and corrupted my mother, but a quiet, warm person who had changed, who now cared about me. God filled me with His new love and joy. All the hatred and anger that used to haunt me through school had melted.

When I returned to Texas, I knew nothing would be the same again. Christ had brought freedom from the chains of resentment. I knew I needed help in my Christian life—I'm that kind of person. By now I had learned that one reason I had hated my mother for betraying me was because I needed people to lean on.

I prayed for Christian friends. One day I drove past a building with "Youth for Christ" on the front, and I called to see if someone could help me. I hadn't found a church to meet my needs. Larry Kreider, the YFC director, visited me and introduced me to Campus Life activities in my school.

This past year has been one of growth. Most of my friends who clung together because of drugs rejected me, but I found a new set of Christian friends in Campus Life. They stuck with me, filling my vacuum of need. And my relationship with my father has grown deeper. He's come a long way.

Mother and Jeff grew even closer to me. They became traveling workers for Youth With a Mission, sharing a transforming Christ with hundreds of people. God had taught me that I can't shrink inside like a turtle in a shell. It's okay to need people, and so I've shared my problems and frustrations with my Christian friends. My old family will never be put together again, and I know I bear the scars from those years. But I've learned to bring them to God. Again and again He's proved Himself as the One we can lean on.

God changed everything. First He changed me, making me more like Himself. Then He changed my sick emotions and fantasies and replaced them with a healthy dose of His love. I'm convinced there is no real life except that which is found in the light of His Son. ■

The Way It's

So many families are messed up, you
better in mind. When you're down
sides. You forget there's
□ There are no perfect families. But
and some ideal qualities you can begin
next three chapters take you to the
the aerial view gives you a better idea

Meant to Be

tend to forget God had something
in a deep rut, you see only the
a big world up above.
here is an ideal you can shoot for . . .
to see in your family right now. The
sunshine above the rut. Sometimes
how to get out. . . .

A Tale of Two Sisters

by Hope Warwick

■ A young father had two daughters.

As the years went by, he watched them grow up through "Captain Kangaroo" and skate boards, the new math, gold eye shadow and a bewildering series of diets. They teased each other, fought some, and increasingly took for granted their life together at 205 Woodfield Place.

One day when the youngest was sixteen, she decided she could do without homework and curfews and the endless mother-daughter hassles over what to wear and who to go with.

Without forgiveness, there'd be no family

So she stuffed an extra pair of Levis into her sleeping bag, cashed in two government bonds she'd been given to save toward college, and hiked about three miles down an abandoned railroad track to the outskirts of town. At dusk, she cut across a vacant lot to the freeway and hitched the first of five rides between her Pittsburgh suburb and New York.

Police couldn't trace her. And every runaway organization her parents managed to contact could give no information.

In the city, she blew all she had on a one-month stint in a dingy hotel and on other unfun things like food, an extra blanket, a red nylon parka, and deodorant.

There was no homework.

When she ran out of money, a group of kids she'd gotten in with offered her a damp corner of their basement room.

She discovered that pot made her sick (dizzy, vomiting sick), and though it embarrassed her no end, she never tried other drugs after that. She discovered, too, that these new transient friends used her as thoroughly and callously as the kids and teachers back home had seemed to.

Her sleeping bag got moldy.

For two weeks she wandered around downtown Manhattan, checking out "Help Wanted, Female" ads, but no luck. She bought a different paper then and sat down at one of the back booths of a greasy pizza joint to read more ads. Her feet hurt . . . both heels were blistered. She had a headache.

She thought about the dark, eight-block walk to her corner room and decided she was going home. So she called her dad, and he wired money for plane fare, even for a taxi to the airport, though she told him she could take a bus.

Early the next morning on board Allegheny's flight 841, she let down her seat as far as it would go and slept deeply.

Her dad had somehow gotten through the Passengers Only gate and he met her on the runway. Not once did he accuse her of hurting him, and she knew he never would.

Out in the parking lot, he led her to a '68 VW.

"You've come down in status," she said. "Did you sell your Buick?"

"No. This one's yours." He gave her the keys and hugged her hard. He was trembling, and she could recall having seen him so deeply moved only once before: when her mom came out of surgery and they said it wasn't cancer. "It could probably stand a paint job, but we thought you needed something to get around in."

Twenty minutes later, she pushed open the back door and walked into the warm, coppery kitchen. Bacon was frying, and the coffee had just started to perk, slowly, with uneven rhythm.

Her sister slipped quietly into the family room, turned on the TV, and sat waiting for the test pattern to fade into an early morning talk show. She felt cheated, pushed aside. The happy reunion chatter in the kitchen ground into her stomach. What did all her attempts at being an ideal daughter mean anyway?

A few minutes later, when her dad came in to call her to breakfast, the nagging hurt inside her spilled out. "Okay, I don't claim to be perfect, but at least I've stayed home and done darn near every cruddy thing you've ever asked, and you never even say, 'Thank you.' I slaved in a restaurant to buy *my* car. Now *she* comes dragging back here, a washed-out little streetsleeper who's blown her college savings and put you through hell, and you—you're *glad!*"

He stared at her for a long time, as though willing her to understand. "Our love for you is stronger than ever. But it's a time for joy! Your sister's back. If we couldn't forgive each other, we'd have no home." (Aspects of this story sound familiar? See Luke 15: 11-32.) ∎

THE TROUBLE WITH PARENTS

Three-Way Love

If love says to God:

I love You . . .

If You guarantee me a clear skin, a few select friends and grades good enough to keep my parents off my back;

If You answer my prayers (a) immediately and (b) just the way I had in mind for You to;

If You don't interfere with my climb toward popularity or cut into the time I need for basketball practice and romance;

If You let me get my way with teachers; parents . . .

There are different kinds of love— but only one really makes it

Wallowitch

by Hope Warwick

If love says to others:

I love you . . .
If you're good-looking enough to
make me proud to be with you;
If you agree with me on politics (both national and small-scale
student level), religion and what's fun;
If you're the right color, wear the right style Levis and do your hair
the way I do mine;
If you smell good;
If knowing you will up my status;
If you feed my prejudices by sharing them.

Because Love

Then there's because love—it's the kind kids and parents specialize in.

Parents say: I love you . . .

because you're a lot like me (ambitious, hard-working);

because you got a job last summer instead of bumming through the whole vacation;

because you make reasonably good grades and keep your room picked up;

because you're going to our *alma mater* next year;

because you usually get home on time and don't do a lot of things to make us worry (as far as we know);

because we approve your choice of friends—*our* kind of people.

Kids say: I love you . . .

because you adjust my allowance when I need extra money for clothes or gas;

because you let me stay out late, and don't ask a lot of specific, nosy questions;

because you respect my opinions;

because you're willing to put me through college without requiring that I adopt your lifestyle;

because you let me have the car whenever I want it (well, usually).

Ed Lallo

Anyhow Love

Because love beats **if love**, but it's still nothing like the kind of love Jesus showed us and wants to pour through us to others.

God's love is anyhow love.

It says
Hang me on a cross and take my life,
Turn away and refuse to listen to me;
Hit me when I disagree with you.
Use me.
Call me nigger, honky, whitey, pig, fanatic.
Cut me down to pad your own ego,
and exclude me from your crowd.
Embarrass me in front of my friends.
Misrepresent me, ruin my name;
distrust me and undermine the trust
others have in me.
Turn my friends against me;
be unfair with me.
Ignore me . . .
              I LOVE YOU ANYHOW.

There is a saying, "Love your *friends* and hate your enemies." But I say: Love your *enemies*! Pray for those who *persecute* you! In that way you will be acting as true sons of your Father in heaven. For he gives his sunlight to both the evil and the good, and sends rain on the just and on the unjust too.

If you love only those who love you, what good is that? Even scoundrels do that much. If you are friendly only to your friends, how are you different from anyone else? Even the heathen do that. But you are to be perfect, even as your Father in heaven is perfect.

(Matt. 5:43-48, *Living Bible*)

Bob Combs

THREE-WAY LOVE

Why I Like My Parents

by Tim Stafford

■ When I think of what makes my family good, I think of report cards. Somewhere between junior high and high school I became—to this day I don't know just why—a very private person. I did not like to tell anyone what I did, who my friends were, or how well I was doing in school. I especially didn't like to tell my parents. I think it was a quiet form of rebellion—of saying, "It's my life, and it's my choice whether to let you inside."

When I think of what makes a family good, I think of report cards

Consequently, from the time I was in the ninth grade until I finished college I never once showed my parents a report card. It wasn't that I was doing poorly in school and was ashamed; I was doing well. But I considered my grades my business and no one else's.

What amazes me is that they never asked. They must have wanted to know. Some of my friends' parents would grill them each day when they got home from school on how they had done. They would want to see each test score, each homework paper. My parents were radically different. Never once did they demand to see my grades. Sometimes they would comment that they learned more about what I was doing from reading the school newspaper than from talking to me. But they didn't press it.

109

The way I was reacting—withholding all information—was almost as immature as getting drunk and throwing beer cans on the front lawn. My parents had the wisdom to see that for me it was necessary—and they respected me by not trying to coerce me into talking.

They did not treat each member of my family the same way. My brother got incessant reminders and questions about his school progress. He needed them. I really didn't. And because I was allowed my own quiet form of rebellion, I never felt the need to rebel in a significant way. I never had to get drunk or run away to prove that I was different from the rest of my family, because they always allowed me to be an individual.

With every year that goes by I learn to appreciate that freedom more, sometimes almost to the point of awe. My family is not perfect, but sometimes, especially in contrast to others I've seen, I begin to think it is very close.

But I'm not writing to gloat, or make you feel jealous. I want you to think with me about what makes a family good . . . what made mine good, and what makes any family what it ought to be. Obviously, not every family should be like mine. Things that suit us would bore other people to tears. We do things our own, odd way. But underneath our oddness is a set of principles I think every family should have.

Acceptance. When my parents didn't demand to see my report card, but let me do things my own way, it wasn't because they *approved* of my silence. They *accepted* it. They knew I was an individual who would have to work out his problems in his own way. They accepted me for what I was.

Some parents rank their kids the way radio stations rank the "top ten." On the other hand, some kids have a "favorite" parent. They play their parents off against each other. Not so in our family. There are four kids in our family, all very different, but there are no favorites. Nor are there black sheep. Some of us make friends more easily than the others; some are smarter; some are better looking; some have accomplished more.

At school that's the way you're often known. "He's slower than his brother." Or, "She's the ugly one." But inside a family that should be unfamiliar terminology. You are accepted as a member of the family, no matter what you do or how you look. A brother or sister or parents may wish you were different; they may point out your failure to you, or, in the case of your mother and father, punish you if you don't respond. But that never means they will reject you if you don't respond as they hope you will. Your membership card to your family is simply the fact that you were born. You belong.

Are there favorites in your family? Do you compare yourself with your brothers or sisters? Do your parents? Does this quality need working on?

Love. Of course, I was held and told that I was loved. My parents expressed their love in all kinds of ways—really, in everything they did. Virtually nothing is more basic to a good family than love.

But perhaps what strikes me most is how my mother would look at me, smile and say, "You are *such* a nice-looking boy. You look especially nice when you smile." Maybe I did look nice to her, but I think what most people saw was a scowling, pimpled mask. My mother didn't scold me for scowling; she encouraged me to smile. She told me how nice I looked, and there was probably nothing I needed to hear more—I felt very ugly.

For doing so she got no reward. I never put my arms around her and thanked her for saying that. At best I would act embarrassed and stalk off. At worst I would tell her in an irritated tone to leave me alone. But she never got tired of telling me how nice I looked when I smiled. She persistently loved me, even when I persistently refused her love. She was really the only person who kept me from feeling hopelessly ugly. She did it without reward, and she did it day after day after day. That is the quality of love you seldom find in a friend, but strangely enough often find in parents. Yet most of us wake up to our parents' love last of all. Long after we have learned to make and appreciate friends, we are still unaware of how unconditionally parents love us.

Does your family love that way? Or do you need to work on it? Do you get built up at home? Do you build up your parents? Your brother or sister?

Sacrifice. It's hard to think of an example of how my parents sacrificed for me. It's hard not because they didn't sacrifice, but because they did it so naturally, without thought. They never told us how much they were sacrificing for us. Sacrifice? I don't think they would have thought of it that way. It was just the way people act in a family.

They sacrificed money. They sacrificed time. They sacrificed their lives. They fed us and held us when we were sick. They put up with our sophomoric smart-aleck talk. They sent us to college. My dad took me backpacking. They might have had only two kids (or none) so they could live in a nicer house, be freer to go where they wanted on vacations, have some peace and quiet. Instead they had four children. I'm not saying they received no rewards for their sacrifice—I know that they loved being our parents, even though it must have been a great pain at times. But with or without the rewards, they unhesitatingly sacrificed their own selfish goals for the good of the family.

From a very early age they expected us to do the same. If the family was going on a picnic, it didn't matter that you had something you would rather do with your friends. A family picnic came before your personal desires. You, too, could sacrifice for your family.

Do your parents resent their sacrifices? Do you resent yours? Or do you gladly, naturally sacrifice?

Priorities. While they sacrificed for us, my parents also kept their priorities straight. When I was very small the subject of choosing between us and my father came up in a conversation with my mother. I can remember the shock. "I love you very much," my mother said. "And I can't imagine how the choice would ever come up. But if it ever did I would have to go with daddy. As much as I love you, I love him more." For a few hours after that I felt very small and lonely. But I always knew, from that time, that my parents' relationship to each other came first.

So did their relationship to God. It was communicated in small ways. If my mother was praying in the morning, she would not stop to help me find my shoes. We *always* went to church on Sunday, even when we were on vacation.

Neither of my parents provided a taxi service for us. We lived quite a long way from school, so we often needed rides to school events. And they were glad to take us, when it was convenient. But they did not drop everything to cart us to various places. We would get rides from friends, or walk, or just not go.

Was it because they didn't love us enough? They made very clear in other ways just how much they did love us. But they also made it clear that their lives were not wrapped around ours. They did not exist as our servants; we did not exist as theirs. They lived first for each other, for God, for the priorities (family included) that God had given them. Even though that meant I got deprived of a few things—help in finding my shoes, or a ride to a meeting of the Math Club—I am grateful for it all. It provided me with a model for forming my own life. And it made it easier to leave them when the time came. They could happily see me go because I was not taking their life with me.

Do your parents lose their own identity in you? Are you encouraged to sacrifice your whole life for "family"? Or is your family's goal that each of you grow?

Discipline. There were rules. There were fewer and fewer rules as I got older, but there were always rules. If you disobeyed them you got punished. As nearly as I can remember, I got punished a lot.

There were chores to do. It was our house, not "their" house where we kids happened to reside. Our parents were working hard to help us, and we were expected to work hard to help them. I don't remember this being a big deal. It was just expected, and we did it. Where it usually becomes a big deal is where it *isn't* expected, and kids get away with murder. Pretty soon they begin to think that the world exists to do them a favor. When they begin to find out that isn't so, it hurts.

Are there rules in your home? Are you expected to do your share, and to behave respectfully? Or do you get away with murder?

Respect. From the time I was a small child, I felt respected by my parents. My opinions mattered. I was never expected to take the ideas my father had and repeat them. In fact, that would have been thought of as rather inferior in my family; we were expected to have our own opinions on politics, on our faith, on the books we read. And it went without saying that anyone's opinion—mine, or my father's—could and should be questioned.

That doesn't mean we functioned as equals. My mother and father ran the house; we did what they said. But they respected us enough to listen to our opinions. They told us what to do, but they never told us what to think. They expected to learn from interacting with us.

In other families respect might work out in other ways. The basic quality is this: though we have different roles—mother, father, sister, brother, daughter, son—we are each made in God's image. God has given each one the right to decide what he wants to think and what direction he wants to take with his life and no family member should try to take away that right. It isn't that parents treat children as though they were adults. But they do treat them as people who are growing to be adults. Their goal is to help their children reach the point as soon as possible where they can genuinely be equals and friends.

Do you feel respected as an individual? Do you respect your parents' individuality?

Challenge. There are families that respect each other so much they leave each other totally alone. Ours was never that. Perhaps we overdid it: it took me quite a while to realize when I told someone at college that a movie they had liked was, in my opinion, really awful, that they might take it as an insult. In my family we were always challenging each other's opinions and actions. Without a solid foundation of love and respect it would have been devastating. As it was, it helped us to sharpen our lives—to really think about what we believed and what we did, and have reasons for them. I feel sorry for people whose families "get along" but never sharpen each other.

Do you feel your family is an atmosphere where people are challenged to think, to reevaluate, to grow in new ways?

Communication. There are many ways of communicating, and only a few of them involve the mouth. A hug may communicate more love than words.

But words do a lot, too. There was always lots of conversation at our dinner table, and it was usually interesting. I remember, too, the late-night kitchen conversations with my mother, long after everyone had gone to bed. She would talk, and she would listen, too. Communication went both directions.

A family can have the greatest love and respect and acceptance, but if they don't communicate that to each other, it all goes for practically nothing.

Is there open communication in your family? Do you really listen when someone speaks? Do you feel others listen to you?

Faith. Maybe the best thing I can say for my parents is that each of their four kids came to know Jesus Christ. That happened despite the fact—and maybe because of the fact—that my parents didn't push their faith. It was part of their respect for us. They required that we go to church, and there was plenty of talk about God in our house. But they were not uptight, the way it must be very easy for parents to be because they know just how crucial faith is.

I can remember vividly a period when I had just started high school, and was feeling grave doubts as to whether I was really a Christian. I didn't even know just what a Christian was. But I was sure that whatever a Christian was my parents were. I could never deny Christ's reality in their lives. They were not rabid gospellers, but they looked at the world—at their home, at their family, their jobs, their money, their children—from a Christian point of view. They were not uptight about any of it because they knew God was in control.

A family that lacks real faith in God not only has no real sense of direction, but it also finds it difficult to both love and relax. Only God can give you the will to love, and only God can give you the security to relax and let Him take charge of things.

Is there a sense of God's aliveness in your family? Or is He as dead as a dictionary? Does He affect everyday life, or Sundays only?

As you've read this list, I hope you've checked it off against your family. No doubt there are superficial things you both like and dislike about your family. You like the fact that you take vacations camping together. You dislike that they insist on a midnight curfew. But how do you like your family when you talk about the qualities under the surface—love, respect, faith? Maybe you found as you read the list that you were saying, "Who does he think he is? My family is just as good as his." Or perhaps you found yourself wondering what you could do to change some areas where a crucial quality was weak or missing.

Either way, it can do you good to think about it. These "underneath" qualities are what count far more than the superficial things. The "underneath" qualities are what families are really all about.

Why did God choose to use families to raise us? Why not have us born fully mature, as many animals are? God could have designed the world nearly any way He chose; would it not be possible for Him to work around the long, agonizing power struggle that often is part of growing up in a family? So many families are bad; wouldn't it be better to do without?

I do not know all the reasons God chose to use families. But I can think of a few. The first is hinted at when Jesus began His model prayer by calling God "Our father." God is not, humanly speaking, our father, but we need a model to help us understand what our relationship to Him is. It is found in the family. (In a few places, the Bible describes God's love for us as a motherly quality, too.) Go through the list of qualities I gave. Don't you find them in God, too?

So one reason God raises us in families is to inform us of what He is really like. Thanks in part to our families, God is not simply an abstract idea, a "Force." We know His personal qualities firsthand because of our families.

Families also teach us how to get along with people. It's one thing to get along with someone at work, or school, and quite another to get along day after day, sharing a bathroom or a bedroom, doing chores, accepting parents' discipline. On that basis, parents' faults come out. Everyone's faults come out. It is not easy to love each other on a day-to-day basis.

Yet relationships are the key to life. It is for loving each other, not for great accomplishments, that Jesus said Christians will be known. It is relationships—in church, at home, at work—that Paul constantly stresses in his writings. And our relationship to God is the basis of our lives.

Families rub off our rough edges. They teach us how to compromise; you can't always get your own way. They teach us how to take orders; our parents are not the last authorities we'll be under. They teach us, ideally, the meaning of love, especially in situations where love is not really easy.

Even a bad family usually teaches more than no family at all. It is a rare family that will totally dump you for misbehaving: they will not fire you the way some future boss may, or drop you as a friend the way someone at school may. Families, even bad families, normally hang on to their members: they continue to feed them and clothe them. And most families provide some kind of loving support, so that the pain of rubbing off edges can be tolerated.

Families aren't *supposed* to be easy. We're not meant to live free from friction; friction rubs off the edges. It is inevitable that in learning to relate to people day-by-day, and in growing into adults, we feel some tension, and some pain.

Granted that your family has faults, what strengths does it have? Of the qualities I listed, how many are relatively strong in your family? Aren't you much better off than you would be with no family at all?

From that perspective you can look for the weak spots. You probably aren't the only one who would like to have a better family—I imagine your parents feel the same way. But perhaps they don't know how to make it better. Maybe those weak spots are really blind spots in their lives. Maybe they had a lousy upbringing that blinded them. Maybe your dad's father didn't know how to communicate love to his kids, so your dad never learned. Maybe your mother's mother nagged her, so she never learned what it means to have respect in a family.

On the other hand, some of the problems are probably due at least partly to your blind spots. It could be that if you talk honestly with your family about the problems you feel, they'll point out aspects of *your* life that aren't helping.

I believe firmly that, with better communication and a strong will to make things better, most families can improve. They will not improve, however, so long as you focus only on the problems. The problems should only be a starting place; the focus should shift toward positive qualities. For instance, rather than complain about arbitrary rules all the time, as though you preferred no rules at all, you should concentrate on working toward a set of rules that encourage you to be disciplined yet also show respect for all the people involved. If you can propose an alternative to the way things are done, and explain why it's better, you're much more likely to get your parents to listen.

Even if you can't change things, focusing on the positive qualities is important. The worst thing you can get from a less-than-perfect family is a negative attitude toward life. If at eighteen or twenty-one you leave your family with a list of all the terrible things that were done to you, you will probably end up doing the same things to other people. If all you think about is how narrow your parents' minds were, your own mind will probably develop a different kind of narrowness.

But if you leave your family with a list of qualities that make a family relationship (or any relationship) ideal, you are headed *toward* something, not simply *away* from something. You are headed toward just the kind of maturity that families were designed by God to produce. ∎

How to

So you understand how your
causing the trouble between you. You
time expressing that. You even
your family to become.
Your parents make the rules.
□Can you change things?
□No, you cannot be absolutely sure
can make a difference. Sometimes the
keep things from falling apart. After a
is mentally or physically sick, you can't
ideally. But at least you can help make
□Sometimes you can be a major
change. A single person willing to love
It takes time, and patience, and
than you now have. But what is more
□The following chapters give guidelines

118

Get There

parents feel. You understand what's
know they love you but have a hard
have a grasp of what you'd like
□ How do you get there?
Can you have any effect at all?
□ The answer is, "Somewhat."
of changing your family. But yes, you
difference you make will be simply to
death or a divorce, or when someone
expect to make your family function
things better than they could be.
factor in bringing about change, major
can sway every other family member.
probably a lot more personal strength
worth the effort?
on how to make it better.

The Five Biggest Hassles

by Jay Kesler

■When I talk to kids who have problems with their parents, I nearly always begin by asking them what they don't like about them. The answers are pretty predictable. I hear five complaints again and again: 1) My parents don't trust me. 2) My parents don't love me. 3) My parents don't listen to me. 4) My parents pick on me. 5) My parents are hypocrites.

I would be just like a parent if I told you to forget it and just do what you're told to do. Those problems do exist, and they're not all your fault. But they're not all your parents' fault, either. Almost any time people have trouble getting along, it's a problem

Trouble with your parents? Don't give up, man. You can train them

built up over a period of time. You can't say, "One is at fault and one is innocent."

I'd like to tell you some things you can do from your end of the problem.

My Parents Don't Trust Me

Many kids tell me their parents don't trust them. What they usually mean is that their folks don't trust them to stay out all night, or take the family car somewhere, or choose their own friends. Those are things everyone wants to be trusted with—their own car, their own freedom, their own friends.

But how do you get to be trusted?

You have to be trustworthy, or "worthy of trust." You have to

121

prove that you're trustworthy to your parents. That may be unfair, but that's the way it will probably be. You do it by starting with little things. If your parents tell you to get home by 11:00 and you're always late, they're going to say, "Well, if he can't tell time, he can't be trusted with something bigger." However, if you call from someplace and say, "Hey, dad, I'm on my way, but it's going to take twenty-five minutes to get home, so I'll be ten minutes late," you'll find when you want some late privileges you'll have a much better chance.

There's a good reason behind this. If your parents are smart, their goal is for you to become independent. They don't particularly want baby birds in the nest all their lives. They want you to fly.

But to fly, you have to develop gradually. You don't go out and challenge the neighborhood cat the first day. You go out on little loops to see if you can do it. The loops get bigger and bigger, and the day may come when you're ready for the neighborhood cat. In fact, if you're really ready for something tough, your parents will enjoy it with you. To get to that stage, you have to excel at the little loops.

Break down another word: "responsibility." It's really "response ability," the ability to respond maturely to situations.

Believe me, your parents watch how you respond to things. Can you respond to money maturely, or does it burn a hole in your pocket? When you are disappointed, do you take it in stride, or do you have to pout about it for a week? Parents watch those things. They're not trying to spy on you; they just want to check your response ability, to see if you're ready for more.

If you really want privileges at home, I'll tell you how to get them. Just start doing all the little, dumb stuff according to the book. Stuff like making your bed, picking up your clothes and being neat, doing the dishes without being hassled into it. Do that for awhile and your parents will be sitting ducks.

Think of it as a game. Parents are trainable. If you're smart, you can work them anyway you want to. It's all how you think of it. Like the two mice talking about the scientist. One mouse says to the other, "I think we've got the scientist conditioned. Every time I push this little lever he gives me food."

One other need: communication. One kid told me, "My parents don't trust me with my friends. They don't like them just because they've got long hair and they think they're trouble-makers. If they

THE TROUBLE WITH PARENTS

knew what the kids they want me to hang out with are like, they'd be glad I have the friends I do."

"But have you ever thought of telling them?" I asked him.

How can you expect your parents to trust you with your friends unless you've told them what your friends are like? If every time they ask you a question you grunt and make them feel like it's none of their business, you're not going to get them to trust your friends.

Kids say, "My mom doesn't trust me."

"Why not?" I ask.

"Well, she reads all the papers and hears about all the things kids are doing, and she thinks that's the kind of thing I'm doing."

"Well, does your mother know anything about you?"

"Not really."

"Why not?"

"I guess because I never told her."

Do you ever sit down and tell your parents what kind of person you really are? What you really want out of life? What your goals are? What your values are? As they see your ideas maturing, they will feel much more confident to say, "He can be trusted when I'm not here."

My Parents Don't Love Me

When kids complain that their parents don't love them, I wonder how much they know about their parents.

I know what my mornings are like. Some people get up every morning and say, "Good morning, Lord." I tend to say, "Good Lord, morning."

Each morning I have conversations with the shower nozzle. From my state of semi-consciousness in the shower it looks like the only friendly thing in the world. I talk to it about my life and the day ahead. I say, "Man, I've got to go to work again, the same job I've been doing every day for seventeen years. There's no way out—it's a life sentence. The kids are eating more; the rent is soaring; the more I make the more expenses seem to rise. Help!"

A million other fathers do that every day. You think your father's trapped in the corporate jungle? You're probably right.

Why does he do it? He could jump in a car, start driving, and never come back. He could desert your family and run around conceiving kids like you. That's fun, you know: no responsibilities. Just how many pleasures is your father treating himself to? Probably not too many.

So why does he do it? The only explanation that makes much sense is that he loves you, and he's determined to take care of you. Maybe he doesn't know how to show his love properly, but he does love you. His intentions are good.

What about your mom? Do you know what she's like? I'll give you some hints. First, go to the cupboard sometime, open the door and look at all the dishes. Then start with the number of days in the year. Multiply that by the meals in a day. Then multiply that by how old you are. That's roughly the number of times your mother has washed that same set of dishes. Think that gets a little boring?

Then look at your clothes. How many times has your mom washed those same clothes? How many times has she folded that same T-shirt? Think that gets a little old?

My Parents Don't Listen to Me

It's amazing that people who live together for years can have such a hard time making intelligent conversation. It works both ways. You should see parents when I tell them this is a complaint kids have. They're amazed. From their point of view, it's you who won't listen to them!

Anytime you're with people who have experienced different things in life, it's hard to make good conversation. It takes creativity and effort. If you interacted with your friends like you do with your parents, how many friends would you have?

Sometimes parents want to talk, but they don't know how. They ask questions no one cares about, like, "How's school?" You know how to break them of that? Sometime just tell them what school is like. Say, "Well, we got there at 8:10 and stood around waiting for the bell to ring. At 8:15 it rang and we went to home room. We sat there for a half-hour and had the announcements and did this and that. Then the bell rang again and we went to math. We were taught all about . . . ." They'll eventually get the idea that a more creative question might help conversation.

I tell parents to try not to ask questions that can be answered simply "Yes" or "Okay." Ask questions that say, "What do you think of?" "What is your opinion about?" The same goes for you as you talk with your parents. Try this one-week experiment. Sit down and think up five supper-time conversations you can talk to your parents about. Then list two or three questions for each meal. "Hey, dad, what do you think about this?" or "Mom, what's your opinion on that?" They'll be able to answer because everyone has an opinion. You may know more about it than they do, but you don't always have to correct them. You're not going to change them anyway. Just listen. Ask, "Why do you feel that way?" or "How did you come to this opinion?" Don't make your parents always end up arguing with you.

Many kids trap their parents into logic that proves them wrong. Don't do that. All it does is get them to say no automatically, because they know you're trying to manipulate them.

And you should practice speaking in sentences rather than grunts. A sentence is very easy to make, you know. You get a verb, stick a noun in front of it and you're in business. Sentences are good because they communicate thoughts. A grunt or an inflection only communicates an attitude, and you can't converse with an attitude.

Another way to get your parents to listen is to tell them once in a while that you need them. Tell them you've failed at something when you have.

I knew a guy who came within a hairbreadth of being hit by a train in the family car. He'd been careless, and it scared him half to death. He was really shook. There was no damage, but do you know what he did? He went home and told his dad about it. He didn't have to, but he did. It was his way of saying, "I make mistakes." In terms of relating to his dad, it was the smartest thing he ever did.

Writing home when you're on a trip is good, too. Even a collect phone call, within reason, won't get a complaint out of most parents. Nothing will warm a parent's heart like knowing you're a little homesick. You might be able to get along without a phone call home, or you may think, "My friends will think I'm chicken if I call." But decide what matters to you most. Do you want your parents to know that they're really loved?

My Parents Pick on Me

I find that a lot of "picking on me" is really caused by a lack of information. Parents want to know what's going on in their kids' lives. Many times kids don't volunteer it. What can a parent do but pick on you?

Maybe your parents are always picking on you about your friends because they don't know what kind of people they are. If Susie Jones, the girl your mother thinks you *should* take out, is a hypocrite, sit down and explain that to your mother.

Kids complain that their parents pick on them about school. The trouble is, they haven't told them enough about school. Once you volunteer information, the picking will let up.

You can eliminate some kinds of picking by figuring out what petty things bother them. What irritates your dad? Maybe it's that you slouch at the table, or he doesn't like your hair in your eyes. Well, is it worth it? Is it worth all those hassles every day for the next two or three years? If you know he gets irritated when you don't respond the first time to something he says, why not just give in and respond right away? Sometimes I think kids try to start a war with their parents. It's not worth it.

Sometimes there are real reasons why your parents pick on you. Did you ever ask them why they care so much about what kind of clothes you wear? It might be that some of the things they say have some reasons behind them. Is it possible that your mother knows something about life that makes her think twice about short skirts? You might try asking her.

One other cause of your parents' picking on you: your independence. Some parents don't understand you're trying to get away from that formless blob called "family" and become an independent person. Your parents probably don't understand why you're tired of being so-and-so's son or daughter. They think you don't like it because you don't like them—they don't understand that you're just trying to find your own identity.

When you just want to be alone in your room, they think it's because you don't like them. When you don't feel like going where the rest of the family is going, they think it's because you're rejecting them. When you want to move out and get an apartment, they think it's because you can't stand to be in the same house with them. That hurts them, so they pick on you. But explain that you're trying to become an individual. Sit down and explain to them as patiently as possible that you love them, but that you have to be known for what you are, not for what they are. It may take them awhile, but I think they'll be able to understand that, especially if you lace it liberally with the statement that you love them and en-

THE TROUBLE WITH PARENTS

joy them. Many parents who pick on their kids are grasping for some kind of assurance of your acceptance. You want them to stop picking on you? Try giving them the assurance.

My Parents Are Hypocrites

I was riding on an airplane, next to a kid in sandals and blue jeans. I started talking to him, and pretty soon I found out he was down on his dad. His parents were total hypocrites, highly involved in the oppressive corporate structure, wrapped up in possessions.

I said, "How come you're flying in this airplane?"

He said it was the fastest way to get where he wanted. I also found out that he paid the bill with a travel card his father had given him.

Now, I don't understand that. Granted, plenty of adults are hypocrites. But who was flying in the airplane? If you're walking across the country eating berries on the way, I respect that. I like the Walden Pond idea. I like the thought of pitching a tent by a creek and eating roots and frogs. That's honest, that's back to the earth, and it appeals to me. We need some of that. But don't tell me about your folks' hypocrisy when your own life is full of it.

Kids say their parents live in a society that doesn't respect people, where corporate monsters devour people. I won't argue with that. But I ask them: "Are you using your parents? Do you see them as saps you should walk on, or slaves that take care of your clothes? If so, I'm more interested in hearing you talk about how you're going to change your own life."

Parents Are Lonely

Most of what I'm saying is this: let's be fair to parents. Let's be at least as fair to them as you would be to anyone you meet at school. You know how unsure you feel when you get around a group of people you don't know? Well, that's how parents feel around high school kids. They don't know quite how to act. Do you blame them?

I try to make some assumptions about everyone I meet. I think you can apply them to your parents, too, because they are people.

I always assume that everyone I meet is lonely. I won't always be right, but I'll be right about 95% of the time.

I assume everyone is frightened and insecure, so I try to do things that won't threaten them.

What would it do to your relationship if you made those assumptions with your parents? What if you made a special point of being nice when they were busy or wound up over something? What if you gave them a compliment once in a while? Try going over to your mother some night when she's doing the dishes and giving her a hug, not to try to get something out of her, but just to say you love her. I'll tell you, the little warm shivers will go up and down her spine.

Lovers do things for each other just because they want to—not because they hope to get something out of it. It just makes them feel good to do it. Did it ever occur to you to do that at home?

There's a scriptural principle here. It's expressed beautifully in the famous prayer of St. Francis of Assisi, who said, "Let me not be loved as much as to love." Do you like that just because it's sentimental? Real love isn't sentimental. You'll learn that if you try to practice it at home. But it does bring happiness, because the only way to get real happiness is to give it away.

Problem Parents

Occasionally parents have deep problems. Most parents, I'm convinced, really love their kids and want to help them. But there are exceptions, and of course every parent has faults of some kind. How do you handle that?

Suppose your dad had only one leg. Would you be angry if he wouldn't run races with you? Not a chance.

Well, suppose your dad or mom has been crippled psychologically by certain things in their youth. Are you going to hold it against them because, say, they were raised in homes where discipline was administered unwisely and they picked up the wrong signals, and now they overdo it with you? If your mom overreacts, could it be because sometime in her life something happened to make her fearful, something she'd never be able to talk about with you?

Will Rogers said he never met a man he didn't like. He didn't say that because all his life he had the incredible good fortune to meet only great people. He meant that if you get to know a person well enough, you can like him, and you can accommodate his flaws. That's true of parents, too. Why look only at the negatives? If they were someone else's parents, you would probably think they were interesting characters.

What's more, there's the possibility of learning from them. Most people learn from positive examples, and that's certainly the easiest. But there is another possibility: to learn from a negative example.

I know a couple of guys who were brought up in a terrible family situation. Their parents were fighting constantly, threatening divorce. The two sons took very different paths. One got all involved in the situation: he'd get in the middle of a fight, or take one side or the other. And the cycle got to him. You see, no matter how much you dislike your parents now, you'll find yourself acting just like them unless you do something about it. That's one of the worst things about a bad home: it creates a cycle that doesn't stop with one generation. That son ended up making the same tragic mistakes his parents made.

The other son, however, broke the cycle. He didn't get involved in the fights: he backed away and did his own thing. He was helpful when he could be, but primarily when things got bad, he backed off. Today he's as together as you can imagine.

Why? Because he worked at learning from a bad situation. Okay, your father is a drunk or your mother is an addict, or your folks are always fighting. It's a problem that can't be solved overnight, and if the person involved doesn't want to solve it, it won't be solved. You're stuck with it, at least until you're eighteen and can make a life of your own.

But don't spend all your time blaming your parents. They're crippled in some ways: the best you can do is be kind. Just say to yourself, "When I get married I'm going to be a little more careful to find the right kind of mate." Or, "When I have a son I'm going to be a better listener than my dad was."

That's tough to be successful at. It takes a lot of maturity. But it can be done.

It's tough to have a good relationship with your parents. Very few people can be completely successful at it. But it can make a tremendous difference in your life. Few things are closer to you emotionally than your parents. When things are bad at home, everything is affected. But when things are good at home, life is much better. ■

Surviving
a Divorce

by Larry Lewis

■ A young man recently told me, "My parents are separating and it looks like they will never get back together again. It seems as though my whole life will be ruined."

Words similar to these are frequently heard today. About one out of every three marriages ends in divorce and in many of these cases children are involved.

It hurts, but it isn't hopeless

If you are one of these young people you already know that whenever there is a divorce there is hurt. Your parents may have a sense of failure and guilt that their marriage did not succeed. They may also experience grief and shock, fear of the future, resentment, self-pity, frustration, even rage.

In fact, their pain can be so great that they may not act toward you as they would under normal circumstances. The father or mother that you have loved may become irritable, resentful, or cruel. You may find that you don't even see much of one or both of your parents a lot of the time.

Your pain is certainly no less than theirs. Divorce may mean separation from familiar surroundings, relatives, church, and stores. Relationships with your friends may be altered. You may have increased responsibilities and financial problems, difficult living conditions, and schooling problems.

One of the most difficult problems you face is how to act toward your parents. Should you reject one and love the other or treat both alike? This problem is compounded if one or both parents try to get you to take sides.

One young person in this bind said to me: "I don't want to hurt either of my parents. But they are forcing me to take sides, and I don't want to, because I need them both." This girl was depressed for more than a year before she began to see that life still had much to offer her.

If your parents have divorced or are in the process of separating, you may be plagued by similar problems. If so, you can ease the damaging effects of the divorce if you will remember some of the following points:

First, maintain contact with both of your parents.

You may have intense feelings of rejection and hostility for one

131

or both parents. This is understandable, for like every child you wish your parents would be in agreement. If they are not, your world is threatened. The result is often anger, especially toward the parent who seems to be the most at fault.

Unfortunately, this hostility is more damaging to you than to your folks. A parent's love for his child is the bedrock on which the child's good feelings about himself are built and out of which will grow his love for others.

To acquire a well-rounded personality, you need to feel close to both of your parents. Hostility will destroy whatever opportunity there is to experience this closeness.

No matter how they treat each other, try to keep open the lines of communication with both parents. Remember that a divorced parent has not divorced his children. Almost every parent wants to feel close to his children, even though he may not be living with them. If you deny him that privilege, you are really hurting yourself.

Second, avoid placing blame for the divorce.

It may appear to you that one parent is more at fault than the other. But the real causes of divorce are very complicated and almost always mutual. What appears true on the surface often is not the case underneath. Since you can't know all the reasons why your parents have separated, you will do well to forgive both and remain neutral.

This won't be easy. Your parents have probably hurt each other in marriage and may unconsciously continue their war after divorce. They may have a struggle to prove who is right and wrong, and try to get you to take sides. To the extent that you can, resist getting caught in the struggle.

Third, you are not to blame for your parents' problems.

Through steps very logical to yourself but mysterious to other people you may arrive at the conclusion that you are responsible for the divorce. You may think: If I had been more considerate of dad, if I had only helped mother more with the work, or had not complained so much, maybe they would have stayed together.

You probably did make mistakes, But so did your parents. Every member of every family makes mistakes and every family has some friction. But the divorce is not the result of the ordinary frustrations that come from living together. The true causes lie much deeper than this. To take the blame on yourself for your parents' divorce is to believe a lie about yourself.

Fourth, you are not an inferior person because of the divorce.

Most of us have some feelings of inferiority that coexist with the good feelings we have about ourselves. A divorce in the family may bring the inferior feelings to the surface and seem to validate them. This may be why many children of divorce seem to lack self-confidence and feelings of self-worth.

Keep in mind the fact that you are not to blame for your parents' problems. Nor are you any less worthwhile because they have divorced. As a child of God you are a unique person, unlike anyone else on earth, but fully equal with every other person.

You are an important and worthwhile person with a unique contribution to make on this earth. God still tells you, "You are precious in My eyes, and honored, and I love you."

Fifth, your future is not ruined.

Some children of divorce may have a fear of giving and receiving love. They may run from a permanent attachment or be cynical about marriage. Some say, "I'll never marry," and avoid any relationship with the opposite sex.

Others do just the opposite and tend to be promiscuous. Some may vent their anger (at their parents) by getting into serious trouble with the law or by fighting the rules of the school they attend.

But it need not be this way for you. With God's help, you can find a new structure for your life. It won't be easy, but you can learn to accept the division of your time and love between parents who live apart. The Lord will help you even accept a stepparent or some other person for the missing parent.

Many others in your shoes have been able to forgive their parents and maintain a good relationship with both. To the extent that you permit God to lead in your life, peace with both parents can be yours. As the Lord says, "Surely there is a future, and your hope will not be cut off." Continue to depend on Him for guidance and your future can only be bright. ∎

The Case of Non-Christian Parents

by Steve Lawhead

■ Imagine this: You are growing up in a very poor family. Stone broke and destitute, you are making it day-to-day the best you can. But cold, hunger, and sickness are never far off. You see your mother and father (and siblings) tightening their belts and facing the bleak future without much hope of any relief. You wish you could do something to help them, but you're as hungry as they are.

One day a very rich and generous man gives you a fortune—free, no strings attached. He does it because he likes you and wants to help. Suddenly you're rich—filthy rich; unspeakably rich. You'll never have to worry any more. So the first thing

To your folks, you're not a happy new Christian— you're as weird as today's cult followers

you do, naturally, is run home and tell your family the good news— their poverty is over; better days are ahead. Only, when you get home and display your new wealth, they all act like you're crazy or something. Your father says, "I don't want anything to do with your funny money! Don't let me catch you with it around here any more!" Your mother says, "It's fine for you, dear. But I can't accept any of it—not now. Maybe someday I'll find a treasure, too." Your brother and sister say the same thing, "So what? Why make such a big deal out of nothing?"

No one understands. Instead, they grimly go on day after day, as

Arthur Tilley

135

deep in debt and poverty as ever before, and all your treasure is worthless to them.

How does that make you feel?

If you are a Christian and your parents aren't, you already know how that feels. You live that imaginary story every day in real life. No wonder a Christian kid's home life can often be an unsavory blend of pressure, frustration, and loneliness. How do you cope?

Loneliness Is a Two-way Street

The loneliness a Christian feels living in a non-Christian family comes from the fact that communication on many levels is cut off. You don't feel free to share some of the most important things happening in your life. Often there is no support for your faith, no encouragement—two things every Christian needs.

When you don't get something at home the easy thing to do is to go looking for it outside; you go to Bible studies, to prayer meetings or Campus Life Club. You want to spend as much time with your Christian friends as possible. This is where most young Christians should step lightly, because too much living away from home makes parents feel abandoned.

Look at it from their point of view. "Everything was fine until you became a Christian, and then, *bam*! Suddenly home isn't good enough for you and you'd rather spend all your time with your Christian friends. What did we do?" they ask.

Anyone in this situation must continually look for new ways to share with his family. You can't read the Bible or pray together, but there are still many things you can do with your family—what did you do with them *before* you were a Christian? It's a good thing to keep in mind that your family has needs that can be filled only by *you*.

Loneliness is a two-way street. It could be your parents are lonely too, now that you're a Christian. If you want support and encouragement from your family, as a Christian it's best to keep the home fires burning. You can't expect your parents to support something that's taking you away from them. If anything, they'll try to discourage it to get you back.

Slow Down, You Move Too Fast

"I'm not allowed to express *anything* in my family—love, hate, joy, anger, or anything," says senior Nancy Parker. "My parents are not Christians and the atmosphere in our home is totally stifling. It's hard to maintain my enthusiasm as a Christian. I love my parents a lot, and I've shared the gospel with them, but they both have neat little arguments I can't break through.

"Dad says it's too easy—that problems aren't solved just by praying a little prayer." So he won't accept it. He wants everything written out and explained down to the last detail before he'll consider any of it. My mother thinks that if she just goes to church it's enough. They both think I'm strange; they think I'm turning into a fanatic because I pray out loud sometimes."

Nancy faces the same frustration many people do—that of trying to relate a new life style to an old family way of life. Buoyed up by all kinds of new feelings and sensations, Nancy wanted to share them with her family, tell them why she was changing and how they could change, too. But she felt stifled and frustrated when they didn't respond.

It's easy to get frustrated when things don't work out the way you'd like. The only antidote to frustration is patience. Changes, especially major life changes, take time. Parents need time to think about what you're telling them. They have probably been thinking, feeling, and acting the way they do for a long time, and you want to upset the applecart altogether. Changing for them is just not as easy as it is for you.

And a parent has to overcome a certain amount of skepticism before following in your footsteps. Remember, they've seen you go through many changes—from milk to solid food, from grade school to junior high, from a person who hates the opposite sex to one who can't stand being at a distance. They've also seen you take up fads and begin hobbies that lasted a month. How do they know this isn't one more fad? Christianity may be on your top ten today, but what about tomorrow? They need to see some stability in you before they can trust their lives to what you're saying. That takes time. But it's time that can be well spent living your faith before them every day (rather than preaching at them), building yourself for the day when they start taking your new interest seriously.

Contents Under Pressure

A Christian living in a non-Christian environment is under all kinds of pressure, some subtle, some not so subtle. Kids notice that as soon as they go against the status quo of their home, pressure is exerted to make them conform.

Your parents view Christianity differently than you do. To them it rocks the family boat. How much pressure you receive is partly up to you, because much of their opinion about the things of God will depend on how you come across. If you come on too strong, or are offensive or arrogant, pressure will be applied to make you cut it out.

Mark White, a student from Seattle, became a Christian and immediately decided to use the strong approach on his family. He came home and preached to them, saying, "Repent! You're going to hell!" His new faith was met with outright hostility. His parents pressured him to give up preaching or leave home.

It doesn't take much insight to see that Mark's method lacked finesse. But, for some reason many new Christians think that's the only way to share their faith. While it might catch people's attention, it usually only makes them mad. Put yourself in your parents' place. How would you like it if the person you've loved and cared for over the years comes home one day and starts telling you your whole life has been a waste, and you had better get it together because you're doomed. The baby whose diapers you changed now informs you that he knows the only true way to live, and everything you've taught him has been wrong. You'd get a bit hostile, too.

Mark was ingenious though. When he saw his first method wasn't working, he cooled it and switched to another technique. He subscribed to a Christian magazine and began reading it himself and leaving it lying around the house in strategic places. Then he waited. Mark never caught anyone reading his magazines, but he was suspicious. So he carefully placed them on a dusty table and checked for finger prints. Sure enough, it was plain that his magazines were being read by his parents, and soon they began asking questions about what he believed. Then he was able to share with them in a way that made much more sense.

Mark felt less pressure from them because he became less of a threat. Of course, you might still feel uneasy for other reasons. But the pressure you feel as a Christian in your own home is related to the way you treat your family as non-Christians.

The Warning

Jesus warned those who would follow Him that He represented a divisive factor in their lives. "Do you think I have come to give peace to the earth?" He asked them. "From now on families will be split apart, three in favor of me, and two against—or perhaps the other way around. A father will decide one way about me; his son, the other; mother and daughter will disagree . . ." (Luke 12:51-53, *Living Bible*). He knew what problems His life would bring to families.

Jesus knows and understands what you're going through. He, perhaps better than anyone else, can comfort you and help you deal with the pressure, frustration, and loneliness you feel as the only Christian in your home. And, happily, through time, patience, and endurance, He can also change things. But remember, He can never guarantee your parents will become Christians: that choice is theirs alone.   ■

Midnight Writer

■ The following letter is real (although the name has been changed). It was written on impulse at midnight by a high schooler with no intention of its ever being published but as a means to grab her parents and cry out, "Look at me! Listen to me! This is the person I am!"

Dear Mom and Dad:

I am writing you this letter because I have a lot on my mind that I want to tell you, and I know if I tried to say it in person I would either break up or get mad. Maybe I shouldn't write it, but I think I should let you know how

When you can't talk honestly to your parents you can always write

I feel about things so we can understand each other better. The subject is our relationship to each other. Since I am writing it—not you—it will be very one-sided, but this is how I feel.

Sometimes I picture myself as a dog on the end of a leash held by you, the masters. The dog struggles to get free, not because he hates his masters (actually he loves them and depends on them a great deal) but the fact that he is *tied* to them makes him want to get away. As time goes on, if he doesn't get free he will do almost anything, even bite his masters whom he loves.

You see me as a teeny-bopper adolescent who can't really feel and think yet. But maybe this isn't how you see me at all. I get the impression that you are so worried about how I will turn out that you will do anything to "protect me from myself." I feel that you want a stereotype for a daughter, not the real thing.

Do you want a "Susanna Goodwill"-type daughter? By this I mean a daughter who is nice, sweet, popular, and in high standing at the church youth group, never causes any problems because she and her parents agree on everything—and most of all, if she has a boyfriend, he is her age and in the same youth group.

There is nothing wrong with this type, except it is not me. It never will be me! I am a person, not just your daughter. Don't you

141

see that you are hurting more than helping?

This brings us to the point of boyfriends. I am not looking for a husband. When I am interested in a boy, it is not because I want a romantic relationship. It is because I need a friend. You say that I have plenty of friends and friendship leads to deeper things. Maybe I just need someone to say, "I'll accept you as you are. You don't have to change for me." Maybe I just need someone I can talk to and share things with. Some friends you can share with and others you can share totally separate things with. Maybe I just need to be told, "Hey, I like you! I enjoy *being* with you. It doesn't matter what people say because I like you anyway."

I don't think any person finds total acceptance at home. That is why we tell things to our friends that we would never tell our parents. That is also why there is a generation gap; we just can't accept each other as we are. You're always trying to improve me. Do you realize how few times you say that I look nice? Sometimes, but that's only when I wear something you especially like, not that I like. (You could even lie a little, just to make me feel confident.)

If I'm not accepted by you, do you think that makes me more confident of being accepted by my friends? If you think I like John only because I am flattered he would even look at me, you're wrong. I care about him. From him I get this acceptance that was lacking here at home. I enjoy being with him. We understand each other. Hard as it is for you to believe, five years' difference in age does not make a whole lot of difference in people. Maybe I like being with him because I can relax and be myself with him. I don't have much hope that you'll change your minds, but this is how I feel.

Now I'd like to talk to you about church. On the retreat I gave my whole life back to God to do with what He wants. I don't know what that is but I'm sure He'll tell me eventually. I also learned that love is the greatest thing in the whole world. Undemanding, giving love. It's pretty easy to love my friends that way, but it's you I'm having trouble with. When I came in tonight, I really didn't expect to be so upset. I'll say again that I'm sorry if I hurt you (and I know I do with my thoughtless behavior). Do you think you could try letting go a little? That way you wouldn't get so hurt. I am the kind of person who must do it for herself, not take a more experienced person's word for it. Maybe I will get hurt but at least it will be because I made the mistake, not anyone else. I will be responsible for my own actions.

THE TROUBLE WITH PARENTS

What a long letter this has turned into. It's past midnight. I hope you can not only read this letter but also read between the lines to get my meaning. I'm going to sign this the way I really feel, the way I have tried to express myself to you.

With much love,
Kathy

■

HOW TO REACH YOUR PARENTS

When you discuss problems with your parents, you often communicate attitudes more than facts. How about suggesting one or more of these reforms?

1. Everyone needs privacy and a chance to think. Rooms should be private—parents' as well as kids'. If you want to go into someone else's room, knock or ask permission. Failing that, how about "Do not disturb" signs, or setting aside a "Quiet room" at certain hours—say, the den from 7:00 to 8:00 every morning?

2. For a week, try beginning every contradicting statement by saying, "That's your opinion, and I respect it."

3. Write out a workable compromise you can suggest to your parents on cars, money, chores, or hours. It saves fighting a fresh battle every time. And your parents are bound to be impressed if you suggest the rules.

4. Set up a weekly/monthly family council. Alternate the leadership so that everyone can bring up the things that are bothering him or her. Make sure you include some positive things, too.

5. If things are really bad, suggest you bring in a third party—a respected adult, a pastor, or even a trained counselor to listen to your differences.

6. Revise schedules so there's one daily meal everyone can make.

7. Agree to quit comparing. You won't compare your parents with other adults, your car and house with other cars and houses, your church with other churches, if your parents won't compare you with siblings, cousins, and friends, or compare your friends with other kids.

Tim Stafford is an editor for CAMPUS LIFE, the largest, most colorful Christian youth magazine in the world. Month by month CAMPUS LIFE Magazine faces into these and other topics, frankly, realistically from a Christian perspective.

To receive a full year of lively, crisp reading, simply check below. If you are not completely satisfied, a full refund is yours. You lose nothing.

☐ Send me a full year of CAMPUS LIFE for $7.90 (a savings of $7.60 off the single copy price.)

Name_____Age_____Sex _____

Address _____

City_____State_____Zip_____

4TWP

Outside the USA, add $1 per year for postage.

Please allow 6-8 weeks for delivery of first issue.

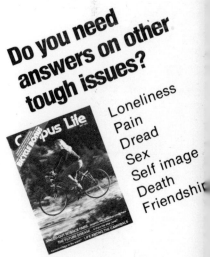

Do you need answers on other tough issues?

Loneliness
Pain
Dread
Sex
Self image
Death
Friendship

Tim Stafford is an editor for CAMPUS LIFE, the largest, most colorful Christian youth magazine in the world. Month by month CAMPUS LIFE Magazine faces into these and other topics, frankly, realistically from a Christian perspective.

To receive a full year of lively, crisp reading, simply check below. If you are not completely satisfied, a full refund is yours. You lose nothing.

☐ Send me a full year of CAMPUS LIFE for $7.90 (a savings of $7.60 off the single copy price.)

Name_____Age_____Sex _____

Address _____

City_____State_____Zip_____

4TWP

Outside the USA, add $1 per year for postage.

Please allow 6-8 weeks for delivery of first issue.

Do you need answers on other tough issues?

Loneliness
Pain
Dread
Sex
Self image
Death
Friendship

U.S. Postage Paid
First Class
Permit No. 78
Boulder, Co.

BUSINESS REPLY MAIL

NO POSTAGE NECESSARY IF MAILED IN THE UNITED STATES

POSTAGE WILL BE PAID BY

Campus Life
MAGAZINE

Box 2720
Boulder, CO 80322

U.S. Postage Paid
First Class
Permit No. 78
Boulder, Co.

BUSINESS REPLY MAIL

NO POSTAGE NECESSARY IF MAILED IN THE UNITED STATES

POSTAGE WILL BE PAID BY

Campus Life
MAGAZINE

Box 2720
Boulder, CO 80322

What God Can Do

by Tim Stafford

■ You can make sure the problems aren't coming from your side. You can change your attitudes, and do your best to understand your parents' feelings.

You can talk to your parents, propose some new ideas, and try to explain how you feel about your conflicts.

And you can take a large dose of patience, hoping that for these last few years at home you can survive your parents' faults, accepting them as human beings who make mistakes.

But you cannot make your parents change. They are unlikely to take advice from you: after all, you were once their baby.

It is not even easy to change your

When all is said and done about what you can do to affect your parents, it isn't much

own attitudes toward them. Powerful emotions constantly upset you (and them) when you try talking calmly to your parents. What ought to be a rational discussion turns into slamming doors and shouting. Sometimes trying to make things better only makes them worse.

But what you can't do, God can. If problems with your parents do nothing more than make you start talking to Him regularly, something good has already happened. The simple act of talking to God each day about your family situation may do more good than confrontations, family councils, counselors, and letters written at midnight.

David S. Strickler

God can help keep your head straight. The worst thing about family hassles is that they're repeated generation after generation. Child-beaters nearly always had parents who beat them. They repeat their parents' mistakes. And so may you.

By praying every day, you renew your friendship with God, who loves you perfectly. You can feel totally secure in His love. You also renew your memory of what's really important. Instead of worrying yourself to death over conflicts with your mother, you remember that ultimately God is in control; what matters is obeying Him, and living a life of love no matter what your circumstances are.

You can specifically pray that God will help you keep your head straight by providing calmness to you, and by leading you to friends who can encourage you and strengthen your faith. You can pray that He will remind you of what is really important. If you do that, day after day, you are more likely to emerge from your family problems unscarred.

God can also directly intervene in your family. He can change attitudes and behavior. You can pray each day that He will work on the people involved—letting them know that He loves them, and helping them to be more secure, so they won't have to take out their fears and insecurity on you and each other. If your parents aren't Christians, you can pray that God will keep bringing Himself to their attention.

But be warned before you pray: God usually works *through* the lives of Christians. If you ask God to change something, the chances are He will want to do it through you. If you ask God to affect your family, He probably will first want to affect you. Don't ask God for anything you are not willing to work to get.

Be warned, too: God may not change your family. He does not magically overhaul things whenever He is asked. Why He doesn't no one totally knows. But one thing is sure: it is through rough spots in your family that God builds character. He teaches you patience. He teaches you how to get along when it's hard. He teaches you realism about yourself. He teaches you to rely on Him. That lesson—reliance on Him—may be the most important thing God can possibly give you. He cares about your relationship to your family, and He wants it to be better. But much, much more, He cares about your relationship to Him. ■

How Are

No two families are exactly alike.
area, weak in another. It's good to
know the
□This final chapter is to help you
and how to improve it. It lists six
and asks a series of questions in that
answers as you go. Then, looking back
your family in that area. Do you need
one you can be
□After each evaluation, there are a
off point for you; you might also want
read and mark suggestions that relate
It's good to know where you are now
getting to where

You Doing?

Your family may be strong in one
appreciate the strong points . . . and
weak ones.
think seriously about your own family
qualities every family ought to have,
area. It will help you to jot down some
over your responses, try to evaluate
to work on it? Or is it a strong area,
satisfied with?
few suggestions. They are a jumping
to flip back to the section you just
to your family's specific weaknesses.
. . . and to have a plan of action for
you want to be.

A Checklist for Evaluating Your Family & Taking Action

Where is your family strong? Where is it weak?

■ No two families are exactly alike. Your family may be strong in one area, weak in another. It's good to appreciate the strong points . . . and know the weak ones.

This final chapter is to help you think seriously about your own family and how to improve it. It lists six qualities every family ought to have, and asks a series of questions in that area. It will help you to jot down some answers as you go. Then, looking back over your responses, try to evaluate your family in that area. Do you need to work on a certain quality? Or is it a strong area, one you can be satisfied with?

After each evaluation, there are a few suggestions. They're a jumping off point for you; you might also want to flip back to the section you just read and mark suggestions that relate to your family's specific weaknesses. It's good to know where you are now . . . and to have a plan of action for getting to where you want to be.

Love

Is "I love you" frequently expressed, either in words or through touch?

Would you be willing to give up some event you really cared about if it were important to one of your parents, brothers, or sisters that you do so? Would others give up something important for you?

Do you find enough time for each other?

Do you encourage your parents? Your brothers and sisters? Do you feel that they try to encourage you?

Is there anything you could do that you feel is so awful you fear your parents would never love you again? Is there anything they could do that would make you totally cut yourself off from them?

What do you think your parents hope you will be when you are an adult? What kind of person? What kind of career do they want you to have? Do they have expectations at all? Are their hopes positive?

Do your parents supply your basic needs, or do you often have to fend for yourself in terms of getting food and clothes?

Does any member of your family seem to want to hurt or destroy another member?

Evaluation: It's fairly unusual for a family not to have love—though it does happen. More commonly, the love isn't expressed well, or isn't understood when it's expressed. For instance, your father may think of going to work as an act of love for you, but you have never understood how he feels about it.

As you go through the questions above, ask yourself, "Do my parents love me? Do the members of our family love each other?"

Then ask, "How well do we communicate that love? Do we try to understand the way each expresses love?"

Action: If you feel there is no love, check your evaluation by talking to the family members you feel have shown little or no love. Be willing to ask, if you can, whether they feel they have love, and how they express it.

Check your evaluation by talking to an older friend of the family, a pastor, or a counselor. (A school counselor can refer you to someone trained to help.) If there is no love, there is probably little you can do at this point to stimulate it. You would be better off to accept that and minimize the hassles, instead of looking forward to someday becoming an adult. A trained counselor can be a great help in working toward that point.

If you feel love needs work, first ask, "Why isn't love better expressed, better understood? Can the causes be changed?" If your mother is an alcoholic, or your father is having problems because he hates his job, it is probably impossible for you to do much to change the situation. Again, a counselor can be a great help in accepting and coping with the situation.

In other cases, you may never fully understand why love isn't better expressed. Or you may think you understand, but realize that things aren't going to change overnight. A father who can't say "I love you" because *his* father could never say it won't learn how to say it instantly. But there can be gradual change.

You can never force someone to love you. But you can do two things:

You can express love to them. People often fail to express love because they are insecure. When you begin to daily practice letting them know you love them, they will probably begin to respond back.

You can let them know how you feel. Be sure you don't accuse: just describe your feelings, and how their actions look to you. This can be done in either a family council or in individual conversation. But be ready to hear how *they* feel about expression of love.

Communication

When you say something that is important to you, do you feel as though everyone in your family listens and tries to understand what you said? When they speak, do you listen and try to understand?

On the average, what percent of conversation at your house is a) complaining, b) encouraging, c) small talk, d) stimulating?

Meals are important times for talking. Do you regularly have meals together? Is there real conversation, or is the TV on? Is everyone in a hurry?

Does your family discuss important topics together?

Do you get new ideas from family members?

When you are feeling down and need someone to talk to, is there someone in your family you would feel free to open up to? Do you think the same is true of other family members?

Wallowitch

THE TROUBLE WITH PARENTS

Evaluation: Checking your answers to the questions above, ask yourself, "Do we have trouble expressing our feelings? Do we have trouble discussing stimulating and important subjects?" Then ask, "Are we just reluctant to open up? Or are there obstacles in the way we carry on family business—like we're always too busy, or the TV is on all the time?"

Action:

Make a list of subjects you would like to see discussed and then think of two open-ended questions to ask about each subject. Be willing to express your own feelings, especially on personal topics.

Practice affirming what is said. Even if you don't agree, try to say something positive about what was said, or how it was said or the fact that it was said at all. If you don't understand, ask for an explanation.

In a family council, bring up the problem of communication. Perhaps you can agree to eat one meal a day together. Perhaps you can take time out from TV to talk, play, discuss a book or the day's news, play the Ungame (a question-and-answer game sold in most Christian bookstores), or have a regular family counsel.

Freedom/Respect

If your mother or father says something that you believe is totally out of touch with the real world, do you usually ridicule him or her? If you said something your family disagreed with, would they attack you or would they merely express their disagreement and begin a discussion?

What qualities do you admire in your parents? In your brothers and sisters?

Are there any qualities in you that your family members let you know they admire?

Do you feel that when you reach the age of 21 your parents will be glad to let you live your own life?

Is each member of your family—parents included—encouraged in hobbies and interests that are not necessarily shared by the rest of the family?

Is any member of your family ridiculed for something he or she does or thinks?

Do you have any privacy?

Evaluation: As you read your answers to the questions above, do you sense that you are respected enough so that you're allowed to think your own thoughts and form your own life? Are you further respected to the point of being admired in some way? Do you respect your parents in the same way?

Action: You can't force anyone to respect you any more than you can force someone to love you. But you can *earn* respect; you can't *earn* love.

What would earn respect in your family? Good grades? A cheerful attitude? Sticking to your curfew? Set out to do it, without making a big deal of it.

Are there specific areas you don't feel respected in? Talk privately to the people involved about how that lack of respect makes you feel. Ask if there is any way you can earn respect in that area.

It's hard to respect someone who doesn't respect you. Do you communicate respect for the way your parents have chosen to live? Do you encourage them in the things they consider important?

Wholeness

Is any member of your family—especially parents—consistently jumpy, nervous, or antagonistic?

Does any member of your family—parents included—frequently withdraw from conversations or activities, either by leaving or by not actively joining in?

Is anyone in your family sick frequently?

Does any member of your family complain a great deal?

Is any member of your family always too busy to talk?

Does any member of your family lack any close friends he or she can talk to about his or her feelings?

Is any member of your family constantly in trouble? Drunk or on drugs? Fighting? Losing jobs?

Do your parents seem to fight and disagree frequently?

Evaluation: If you answered yes to any of the above questions, it could be that is where the family problems stem from. It is hard for someone to function as a good parent, brother, or sister if he or she doesn't feel capable of functioning as a human being. Any real improvement of your family has to involve accepting the fact that he or she has trouble living as a whole person, and finding a way to help.

Action: Talk to the person, if possible, who you think is having trouble. Ask questions and try to find out how he or she is really feeling. Try to find out how you can be more supportive and encouraging.

If the person really seems troubled, check your evaluation with someone else. Talk to the other parent, or to a pastor or counselor whom you trust to keep things quiet and give good advice.

Make up your mind to accept less-than-perfect behavior from the person who seems to be having trouble.

Encourage the troubled person to get professional counseling.

Discipline

At your house are chores shared relatively equally, or do parents or certain brothers or sisters do most of the work?

Are there rules?

Are the rules clearly stated?

Do you feel the rules are basically understandable and fair?

Do you feel that your parents listen to you and are willing to consider your opinion before telling you what to do?

Do you feel that, over the course of time, you are learning more how to think for yourself and how to make your own decisions?

Evaluation: Referring to the questions above, try to decide whether you are underruled or overruled. Also ask, "Is the point of the rules clear? Do I understand how they are supposed to help get necessary work done, or help keep me safe, or help me grow more mature?"

Action: Consider asking your parents for a family council to discuss specific rules.

Writing out the rules as you understand them, and go over them with your parents to make sure you understand.

Asking for help in disciplining your life (homework, getting enough sleep, getting to school on time, etc.) if you think it's needed.

Asking for a merit system, wherein you can earn certain freedoms if you act responsibly. For instance: can you stay out late one night a month if you make it in on time the other nights.

When problems arise, can you pray together? Can you agree to pray separately?

When problems arise within the family, do you basically want the same resolution, i.e., family harmony, better self-understanding?

Faith

Does your family share faith in Jesus Christ?

Is God a daily source of strength to your family?

Do you go to church together?

Religiously, do you feel your parents are most concerned with what you do (go to church, pray, not swear or drink) or what you are?

Are you able to treat your parents as people who are not perfect, but are human beings who make mistakes like you?

Evaluation: Does your family have faith at all? Or is the faith latent, needing to be developed and come out more?

Action: In a family, a "witness" can't be effective with just words. If you don't act in a manner that's helpful, your parents will never accept your faith. Therefore:

Don't let your faith be in conflict with family loyalty if you can avoid it. Do go to church regularly, even if your family doesn't; don't insist that your family's church is worthless or that you can never go to family events because there's a prayer meeting somewhere. Faith should help your family come together, not divide it.

Obey family rules as much as you possibly can.

Communicate as much as you can with your family, even if you don't always get a response. Don't preach or make a long speech; just tell what you are thinking and feeling, both positive and negative.

If possible, ask for a family council where everyone is encouraged to talk about what he believes in, and where he wishes he had more faith. Don't argue; affirm whatever is good and keep your mouth shut the rest of the time. Otherwise you'll sound self-righteous to your family, whether you are or not.

Move closer to God yourself. If it's really doing good things for you, your family will realize it eventually. ■

DATE DUE